THE MOMMY
SURVIVAL GUIDE

MAKING THE MOST OF THE MOMMY YEARS

Barbara Curtis

BEACON HILL PRESS
OF KANSAS CITY

ISBN-13: 978-0-8341-2280-2
ISBN-10: 0-8341-2280-4

Printed in the
United States of America

Cover Design: Chad Cherry
Interior Design: Sharon Page

Library of Congress Cataloging-in-Publication Data

Curtis, Barbara, 1948-
   The mommy survival guide : making the most of the mommy years / Barbara Curtis.
      p. cm.
   ISBN-13: 978-0-8341-2280-2 (pbk.)
   ISBN-10: 0-8341-2280-4 (pbk.)
   1. Mothers—Religious aspects—Christianity. 2. Motherhood—Religious aspects—Christianity. I. Title.

BV4529.18.C89 2006
248.8'431—dc22

                                                          2006026188

10 9 8 7 6 5 4 3 2 1

To my family—
you taught me everything I needed to know.

CONTENTS

Anything can happen, but God will be there too.

The sooner you surrender, the better.

I USED TO BE NORMAL

ONE

Once upon a time I was a pretty normal mom. But that was before I ended up with 12 kids.

When did I begin to change? Was it with Number 3? Number 4? Maybe Number 5. I don't know. For a while, with babies arriving every 15 to 20 months, it all became a blur.

And yet at the same time it all became clear, as though I could finally see what was the important part of being a mommy. So many things I thought really mattered turned out not to matter at all. And so many things I hadn't thought of turned out to be the most important things of all.

Today I often hear, "I could never have a lot of kids. It's OK for you, though—you're so patient [calm, organized—whatever]."

That's not how it happened. I didn't start out patient, calm, organized, or whatever at all. Actually, it was through years of living with so many kids that I eventually became those things I might never have become otherwise.

It certainly wasn't because I'm anyone special. It was simply a matter of survival.

See, with one or two kids, your life has to change only a little. OK, I know what you're thinking, you moms of one or two—that your lives have changed enormously. But it's all a matter of perspective. Remember: I was also once a mother of one (for six years) and then two (for eight years) before my third child was born and the fun really began.

So I *do* know what it's like.

But there has to be a reason that every megamom I've ever met has said, "Once you have three, you could have 20—it's all the same," or something along those lines. And the reason is this: every mom with three or more kids has had to surrender, big time.

From manicures and pedicures (even homemade) to ideas of what constitutes a decent dinner or well-set table —all those things we thought essential to our worth as women are yesterday's news. Once a family's parental units are outnumbered by the kids, things just have to change. And mommies discover that the sooner they let go of some old ideas, the sooner the pressure and frustration disappear and they can begin to enjoy the job.

So if megamommies seem different, it's not that we're heroes. We've just thrown in the towel, too worn out to fight for our rights anymore. Patience, calm, organization— they're just part of our survival kit.

That isn't to say that everyone should have three or more kids. And I truly hope it won't scare anyone away from it either.

While hundreds of parenting books and programs out there offer to teach you a better way to raise your kids, most of them fail to recognize that it's not just about changing your kids' behavior—or even their hearts. You can use all the strategies and methods you want to try to get your kids to change, but the bottom line is this: unless you're willing to change yourself, you're not going to make any progress at all. In fact, if you remain the same self-centered person (now calm down and hear me out) you've been all your prechild life—because marriage may give you a shock to your system but it doesn't hold a candle to motherhood—then you'll end up frustrated and frazzled. Yes, you may have some happy moments, but don't you want more than moments?

In *The Sound of Music*, after Maria has finally admitted to herself that she loves Captain von Trapp and returned to marry him and raise the children, the oldest daughter, Liesl, asks her how she can be sure she loves him. Maria says, "Because I don't think first of myself anymore. I think first of him."

I love that way of putting it: *I don't think first of myself anymore.*

The whole motherhood journey—and now that I've been on it for 36 years, I really do think of it as a journey—seems mostly to center around that issue. Can I care less about myself and more about them? I know there are magazine articles and books aplenty urging you to "be kind to yourself," "take time for yourself," and all that—but I can't help but think of all the mothers throughout the world and throughout history who never had the luxury of even thinking about such ideas. Our culture has really cultivated a sense in us that we're somehow entitled to excitement, beauty, fun, and romance long after we've settled into raising a family. And that sense of entitlement battles against the very real demands of raising children and raising them well.

The tender love we experience when we meet our first baby can wear thinner than we expected when that squalling bundle of needs comes up against our own self-centeredness, our desire for a good night's sleep, or just a little peace and quiet. Nothing can quite prepare you for that—nor for the loss of your autonomy. It's just gone. From Day One of motherhood, you belong to someone else.

What happens then?

In my near-breaking moments, I've always found it helpful to remember James Dobson's definition of love, that it's not a feeling but a *commitment*. So sometimes I may not *feel* very loving, but I'm *committed* to loving. Reminding myself of this, and many other things, has helped me survive as a mother and a human being.

So, yes, motherhood will change you—if you let it. And believe me, you do want to let it change you, because when you've refined the art of not thinking first of yourself, you will very much like the person you become. Plus, you'll experience so much more joy and satisfaction from your life with your children.

I didn't know this at first, of course. It took 36 years of bringing up 12 kids (and I still have six at home, including three we adopted) and more mistakes than I wanted to make to fine-tune my mothering. But you don't have to wait that long or work that hard.

The bottom line is this: no matter how many children you have now—even if you're just expecting your first—you can use some of my survival tips to find the balance and joy in motherhood from the very start.

How I wish I had reexamined my attitudes about sleep, for instance, before my fourth child! It would have saved me a lot of frustration. Instead, I muddled through many demanding nights of feedings, wet beds, earaches, tummy aches, bad dreams, and sleepwalking (once the doorbell rang at three in the morning, and I opened it to find four-year-old Matt, who had no idea how he had gotten there), fighting for my right to eight hours of sleep or mourning the loss of it.

Now I know the meaning of sweet surrender. It's so much easier to be awakened at night if you never expected to sleep eight hours anyway!

And if you do get eight hours now and then, you never knew how grateful you could be.

Inspiration

The mother's heart is the child's schoolroom.
—Henry Ward Beecher

The art of mothering is to teach the art of living to children.
—Elaine Heffner

What children take from us, they give. . . .
We become people who feel more deeply, question more
deeply, hurt more deeply, and love more deeply.
—Sonia Taitz

*A mother is not a person to lean on but
a person to make leaning unnecessary.*
—Dorothy Canfield Fisher

*If you bungle raising your children, I don't think
whatever else you do well matters very much.*
—Jacqueline Kennedy Onassis

The phrase "working mother" is redundant.
—Jane Sellman

*People who say they sleep like babies
usually don't have them.*
—Leo J. Burke

A baby is God's opinion that the world should go on.
—Carl Sandburg

 MOMMY POWER

What's a Mother's Work Worth?

On May 5, 2005, *USA Today* reported that Salary.com, a corporate compensation advisor, had calculated the annual value of the work America's 5.4 million stay-at-home moms do: $131,471.

In their calculations, Salary.com used a hypothetical stay-at-home mom with two school-age children and categorized her work into seven main job descriptions: day care center teacher, van driver, housekeeper, cook, CEO, nurse, and general maintenance worker.

Salary. com assumed—get this—a 100-hour work week of six 15-hour days and one 10-hour day!

Well, at least they got those hours right!

MAKING PEACE WITH
SLEEP DEPRIVATION

TWO

"Is she sleeping through the night yet?"

Isn't that the first thing everyone wants to know about your baby? And so the pressure begins. You're tired and vulnerable anyway. You would do almost anything for eight hours sleep. And so you start to get into the goal-fixation mode too.

A word of advice: don't even go there. If you're blessed with a baby who sleeps through the night, that's great. But beware the frustration that comes from striving for something that just isn't compatible with how God built babies to grow.

Every child's developmental timetable is different. Even though a neighbor's baby—or your last one, even—slept through the night from the age of two months, your new little sweetie may take five or even six times longer. Mommies just have to learn to roll with the punches.

And here's a heads-up: this is just the beginning—of learning to roll with the punches, I mean.

If your baby was born prematurely, if he or she had a

low birth weight or is having difficulty gaining weight, the baby will simply need more food more often. Every feeding will put your baby closer to his or her ideal weight—and so less likely to wake at night. So think on that when you get up for baby's midnight—or two or three A.M.—snacks. More feedings equal more weight equals closer to sleeping through the night.

Some babies are just more high maintenance than others, though few reach the extremes of my seventh, Sophia, whose desperate daddy would throw his coat over his pajamas and take her for midnight rides down country roads to lull her to sleep. So count your blessings next time your baby needs just a feed or a cuddle—it could be worse if the baby demands a car ride!

In the first year, it's almost impossible to spoil a baby, and many authorities—including me—think that if you meet the security needs of the first year, your baby will have a secure foundation, and you'll avoid issues later on.

This isn't to say that once your baby is sleeping in a crib you should jump up every time he or she stirs. Sleep studies show that infants have more and shorter periods of deep sleep interspersed with light. Your baby needs to learn to handle these nighttime ups and downs. Let your baby try to comfort himself or herself back to sleep before you rush in.

But letting a baby cry for long intervals is not appropriate at this age. We need to be cautious about imposing all-night sleep on a baby who—for whatever reason—is just not ready.

The dependence God built into babies has a more subtle and important purpose. In learning to be sensitive and responsive to our babies' needs, mommies learn to sacrifice, to let go of our own selfishness. It's an opportunity to become more like Christ, part of God's plan for us and our development too.

And, as I said earlier, it's just the beginning of more surrenders to come.

 ## HERE'S HELP!

Sleep Sound in Jesus (Sparrow/Emd) is Michael Card's original collection of beautiful baby music, unsurpassed by any I've ever heard. An ICU nurse tucked it into my hand as I hovered by newborn Jonny's incubator shortly after his birth. As I played it for him, it gave me great comfort. Later I found it had been released just the month before. Now it has played for 13 years through four more Curtis babies. My favorites: "Even the Darkness Is Light to Him" and "He Grants Sleep to the Ones That He Loves," both based on scripture.

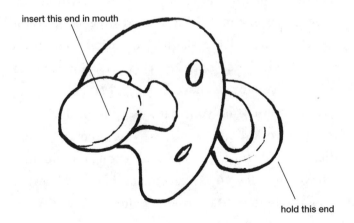

insert this end in mouth

hold this end

Calming a Cry Baby

Harvey Karp, author of *The Happiest Baby on the Block: The New Way to Calm Crying and Help Your Baby Sleep Longer*, recommends the Five Ss:

- Swaddling: Wrap the baby snugly in a blanket, arms inside too. This recreates the baby's experience of the womb.

- Side position: Lay your swaddled baby on his or her side, which aids digestion and is more secure. You can roll up a baby blanket to put in front and back of your child.

- Shushing sounds: Say "shhh" as loudly as he or she cries, or run the dishwasher. This sounds similar to the whoosh of blood your baby heard in the womb.

- Swinging: Rocking, jiggling (not shaking)—and yes, even car rides—recreate the prenatal feelings suddenly withdrawn from the baby upon leaving the womb.

- Sucking: "Sucking has its effects deep within the nervous system," notes Karp, "and triggers the calming reflex and releases natural chemicals within the brain." Well, there you have it—a scientific explanation for what mothers have known all along!

If you've been letting your baby sleep a lot during the day, for housework's sake, perhaps, you need to rethink your priorities. Try to give your baby enough stimulating hours during the day to make him or her need rest at night. Now is one time to begin the major surrender of letting the housework go.

However, if you know you'll probably be up at night, try to get a catnap or two during the day when the baby sleeps. And go to bed early!

FIRST-BABY BLUES

THREE

I remember when my friend Debbie had her first baby. Three months into motherhood, she called me, frantic.

"OK, I fed Daryl and gave him a bath and put him on his blanket and showed him each of his toys, then put him in his baby swing for a while. And now he's been in his bouncer for half an hour. I can't think of anything else to do with him."

I'm really not kidding. Debbie was feeling the responsibility of motherhood in a mighty way. Maybe it was because she was a bookkeeper by trade (which she continued to do from home as a stay-at-home mom), but she seemed to be adhering to some kind of mental ledger, checking off the hours as they passed.

I wished she had called me sooner.

The biggest burden for firstborns must be that they are smothered with attention from their newbie parents. They receive a lot of discipline and a lot of affirmation and praise. Every other child who comes later will reap the benefit of the years when their parents were testing out their best ideas on parenthood with the oldest. But is it any wonder that oldest children grow up to be type-A personalities, workaholics, perfectionists—people who are driven to achieve? Consider: Eleven United States presidents and a whopping 21 out of 23 astronauts were firstborn or only children.

Take it from me—a firstborn married to a fellow firstborn. People always ask how I accomplish so much. What they don't realize is that I really don't have much of a choice. This is part of who I am. I would rather work than play, rather accomplish something than take time to relax.

As adults, oldest children have to struggle to let go of their compulsive behavior—when I was younger, I used to insist that my family clean our house every night before we went to bed—and the desire to control all aspects of our lives. However, I must say that having a lot of kids and raising them past their teens will help you let go of that one real fast.

So when Debbie posed her question, I already knew that being the oldest is a blessing and a curse. Although I would rather be oldest and an overachiever, I sometimes feel shortchanged because I don't have the slightest idea of how to just let things go and have a good time. When I see how gifted my smack-dab-in-the-middle children are at having fun, I wonder if I'm missing something after all.

But I won't dwell on that.

My friend Debbie never had any other children. That little baby she was trying to entertain is on his way to playing baseball in the Major Leagues someday.

And to think it all started with her working so hard to manage his day!

At the time, I just laughed and told her to relax. "Debbie, you don't have to *do anything* with Darryl. Just put him on a blanket with his toys beside you in your office and go to work on your customers' books. He'll keep himself amused. That's what babies do."

Now you and I both know that's not what babies do all the time. But it's what most do most of the time. And it's not really a good idea to interfere with that process.

I mean, of course, it's fine to have playtime and to watch Mommy blow bubbles and listen to her sing and enjoy playing pat-a-cake. But part of what your baby is sorting out is that he or she is a separate entity. Your child is actually already learning to become independent. The time between feedings is growing. Your child is learning that you come when he or she cries, is exploring the extremities of little hands and feet and seeing what things feel and taste like when put into the mouth.

So much work, so little time!

Any non-life-threatening steps your child takes toward independence are wonderful. So you want to be increasing the time your baby can amuse himself or herself. If you put your baby on a blanket with favorite toys just out of reach, this will create motivation to move and to roll and to push forward in the first stages of crawling. If your little one gets a little fussy and you wait a few moments to respond, your baby will have some time to work out of it.

These are good things. These are really the things we do with our children further down the line, and those children grow up reasonably sane and usually far more content than the first. Actually, studies show they grow up to be well-liked, friendly people—many known as peace-makers.

The youngest. Well, we don't really know which is the youngest until the end. I know my youngest birth child, Maddy, fits all the stereotypes. She's optimistic and loves to be center stage.

The truth is that though birth order does affect our children in certain ways, we can be on the lookout for extremes and do our best to help our kids reach their positive potential while strengthening them against the negatives.

As for what to do next with your baby, just remember this: You don't want to be doing science projects for your 13-year-old, and you don't want to be writing college essays for your high school senior. Parenthood is all about inspiring and equipping the members of the next generation so we can pass the baton. It's never too early to start.

Parenthood is the one job you should be working yourself out of each day!

MOMMY POWER

God did not make us from cookie cutters, and there are always wide variations between children, but studies show that birth order does produce certain general tendencies in kids. I found that knowing these helped me understand not only the positive and negative tendencies—and they're just tendencies—of each of my children but also their interaction with each other.

Oldest and only children tend to be

Leaders

Good students

Conscientious workers

Perfectionists

But they may
Have trouble accepting others' mistakes
Worry too much
Over-commit

Middle children tend to be
Well-liked, popular
Able to deal with all kinds of people
Patient and tolerant
Loyal
But they may
Overlook problems
Lack motivation
Put friends before family

Youngest children tend to be
Cheerful and charming
Fun-loving
Good team players
But they may
Play helpless
Demand attention
Resent authority

 ## HERE'S HELP!

In the months following the birth of your baby, there's a lot to deal with. But what about you? Many women's postpartum experience is more difficult because of feelings of disappointment with the way the birth process went. One mother who planned a natural birth may have needed an emergency Cesarean; another who was dead-set against drugs may have needed them after all. In other words, in addition to the regular postpartum issues, moms have to deal with falling short of their own expectations for themselves.

Here's what William Sears and his wife, Martha, say about this in *The Birth Book:*

> Unresolved birth memories have a way of gnawing at your insides, affecting your sense of who you are. What happened at

your baby's birth can influence your feelings about yourself during the postpartum period and for the rest of your life. Unpleasant memories from past births often resurface to infect subsequent births. It's healthy to confront the fact that you failed to have the birth you wanted rather than pretending it doesn't matter, so you can deal openly with the feelings of loss.

A good place to get started is "Making Peace with Your Birth Experience," a lengthy article at the La Leche League web site: <http://www.lalecheleague.org/NB/NBMarApr02p44.html>.

IT'S THEIR HOUSE TOO!

FOUR

Imagine living in a home where all the pictures hang three feet above your eye level, where kitchen counters are mysterious surfaces where you just know all kinds of exciting things are going on that you can never see.

Imagine having to climb onto a chair whose seat is 54 inches off the ground and feeling lost in the bigness, perched at the edge with your feet dangling in midair.

Imagine a world where those in charge bend down to talk to you—looking for all the world as though seen through a fish eye lens—and sometimes even point a finger in your face for emphasis.

That's the world kids live in. Could that be part of their frustration? And understanding that, don't you want to make it more comfortable for them?

While some parents try to live their post-childhood existence with as little impact as possible on their previous way of life, I say that's just not realizing the full potential of parenthood and the building of a family.

If part of the parenting process is learning to be less self-centered, to put the needs of others before our own, the sooner we surrender the better for our children—and, believe it or not, the better for us.

You can start by toddling around your house on your knees and seeing everything the way your child sees it. Those knees are important, too, for whenever you can, kneel down at your child's level to address him or her rather than looking down or bending over.

Empower your child with a stool or two around the house. The stool enables your child to get up to the kitchen counter or wherever Mommy is busy to share some good-quality time.

The point is that from the get-go you want your child to be as involved as possible in the life of the house, both recreationally and with the work there is to do: cooking, cleaning, ironing. (My 12-year-old Maddy was dying to learn how to take over the ironing from her older sister Sophia and still hasn't grown tired of it. Hopefully, you'll have one like that in your crowd too). A toddler can easily scrub vegetables and even learn to peel them if you take the time to think through how it's done and then show him or her in a sequential manner. Even if you're making up busy work—handing your child a damp cloth to wipe down the cabinet doors, for instance—it's the principle that counts: it's not so much that you need the child's help (although you'll certainly need it later as you both grow older), but your child needs to feel that he or she is an important part of the family and is making a contribution. This feeling of self-worth that's being learned can't be replaced by watching a purple dinosaur who sings about loving him or her.

While it's tempting to shoo the kids off to some form

of electronic entertainment when it's time to make dinner, try to avoid that impulse. Instead, keep them involved in the food prep process. Teach them, working side-by-side.

While this may not come naturally, I promise you that you'll be glad you made this investment in your children. The thing is, little children are eager to help. When we keep saying no because we're too busy or we think they're not ready, we turn them off to work, period. It's much better to seize the window of opportunity and open it wide.

Oh, you want to set the table? That would be great! Let me show you how one place looks, and then you can do the rest.

Oh, you want to put away the silverware? Well, I think it's a good time for you to learn!

When we meet our child's desire to learn when he or she is eager and ready, we express our confidence in him or her. Our child's learning will be a joyful experience, and the child will grow up loving to learn. And if what our child is learning about is service—making a contribution to the family—then the child will find it easy to serve as an adult.

In addition to making your little one feel like an important part of the family through affording opportunities to serve, be sure to provide for comfort and needs based on the child's smaller stature.

A coat rack that's at child level by the door provides the ability to get his or her own coat when going out and to hang it up when coming in. Children's closets should be modified so the rod is low enough for them to pick out their own clothes in the morning.

When my first daughter was young 30-some years ago,

it was difficult to find child-sized tables and chairs outside preschool. Nowadays you can pick them up anywhere. Children need a table and chair that's just the right size for them. That's where they can draw, color, do puzzles or manipulatives. And don't put the table away in the child's bedroom. Put it out in the family room or wherever the family spends the most time.

In fact, I think the best pattern for families to set up their homes is with bedrooms made for sleeping and quiet reading. As your children grow, avoid the tendency to put computers and television sets in bedrooms. Keeping them in the common family areas will protect your kids from temptation and encourage more together time. In fact, even with a big family, we purposely have limited ourselves to only one television set in order to encourage family togetherness. Television programs are less passive if you watch and talk about them together.

Jesus said "Whoever welcomes a little child like this in my name welcomes me" (Matt. 18:5). I know that when I welcome adults I take their needs into consideration and try my best to make them feel comfortable and welcomed. It's really just another place for parents to practice the Golden Rule—making their children feel welcome in their own homes.

MOMMY POWER

Besides setting up your home to provide for your children's needs and make them more comfortable, you can pave the way to their becoming better helpers with just a little thinking outside the box. Try moving your dishes from the upper cabinets—where they're custom-

arily kept—to the ones within your children's reach. Now they can un-
load the dishwasher and put dishes away as well as getting out dishes to set the table.

 MAKING CHANGES

Kid-Friendly Art: Start early to give your children an appreciation for
art simply by framing cards or small prints of classical paintings and
hanging them at kids'-eye level throughout the house. By the reading
nook, put pictures like Fragonard's *Girl Reading.* By the coat rack, hang pictures of outdoor scenes like Renoir's *Girl with a Watering Can.* Throughout the house you can scatter pictures like Homer's *Snap the Whip* and Van Gogh's *Starry Night.* Use anything you—looking through the eyes of a child—find appealing. You can find these in greeting card racks,

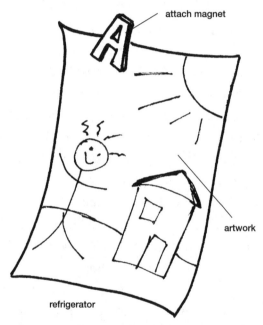

boxed note card sets, or a book of cards that's part of a total art
program for kids called *Mommy, It's a Renoir!* available at
<www.amazon.com>.

IT CAME TO PASS
—NOT TO STAY

FIVE

Our sixth child graduated last summer. Remember—I've been at this a long time! That means six down and six to go. I know if your children are all young, a graduation may seem like something a long time down the line. It isn't. Time will go by faster than you can imagine, and even if you're still getting up at night to nurse a baby, soothe away a tummy ache, or comfort the victim of a bad dream, it won't be long before you're helping them fill out college applications.

I'm now entering that stage of motherhood in which I'm closer to the age of the grandparents who are attending graduation. It's not the most comfortable place to be, since all the other mothers are looking much more glamorous than I. And, yes, I know I'm not supposed to care, and that only makes me feel guiltier that I do.

But let's talk about Zachary, the graduate, because it was his day. And I think knowing a little more about Zachary will give other mommies—even if you're still in the throes of getting a good night's sleep—something sweet to build your dreams on.

Zachary was the fourth of a string of four boys born within five and a half years. When he was two months old, we moved from the suburbs to the country. A couple of weeks later, I broke my arm while flying a kite (that's another story) and had a cast from my knuckles to above my elbow—not exactly the cuddliest situation.

Zachary was a quiet baby, so quiet I would have worried about him if I hadn't been so busy unpacking with one arm. He loved the mobile of yellow duckies above his changing table and flailed his arms and legs in appreciation of them. I would stand by, camcorder in hand, for half an hour at a time waiting for some sound to emerge—you know, talking to the yellow duckies. But Zachary was a man of few words.

He was a very late reader. I taught my other kids to read by four or five, using the very simple but effective Montessori method, but for Zachary, reading didn't click until he was seven or so.

Being the youngest, Zach often found himself with the fuzzy end of the lollipop. Then he would track down Tripp or me to announce with great seriousness, "Mom, Dad, I have to report that my brothers will not let me participate, though I'm perfectly qualified to play the game they're involved in."

By nine he was reading heavy tomes about ancient and modern warfare, biographies of famous leaders like Winston Churchill and Attila the Hun. He had a deep voice and spoke in a dreary monotone, kind of like Eeyore.

And he had a stutter that would disappear for a while only to return.

Not wanting to give it too much energy, I came up with a plan (see the end of this chapter) and stuck to it for five years, watching the stutter come and go. Then one day when Zachary was 10 or so, I wondered when was the last time I had heard it. Like so many other problems, this was just another one that "came to pass"—not to stay.

Zachary turned out to be so intelligent that at 12 he scored 1020 on the SATs. At 13 he passed the California High School Proficiency Exam and enrolled in college.

But when we moved to Virginia, he and his brothers went into public high school. Zach ended up graduating only a year early at 17. But if you asked him today, he would tell you it wasn't wasted time at all. Zach is such a serious student that he can get something out of any course. And our county schools and teachers are very impressive. Plus this last year a wonderful thing happened for Zachary: he really came into his own socially, with friends here, there, and everywhere. He finally felt comfortable inside his skin.

He was the only National Merit Scholarship finalist out of his class of 363 (SATs now 1520). I was so proud of him I could have burst my buttons!

So please don't judge me harshly for bragging so long and so loud about this very special son. For one thing, I want you mommies to know how important it is to relax when your kids are young and not get hung up about problems like stuttering. When I look back, I realize Zach's little brain was probably just going so fast he couldn't get everything out.

And I also offer Zachary as evidence against the charge some people make that kids from big families are dumbed down because of lack of attention from their parents. Zach was 6th of 12—right in the middle. When Zach was four, Jonny was born with Down syndrome and a bunch of medical problems that kept us going in and out of the hospital for 15 months. When Zach was 5, Madeleine was born. When Zach was 7 we adopted another baby with Down syndrome. Mama started writing. Then there were two more adoptions.

It's not as if we were grooming him to be what he turned out to be. But I believe that when God plants something special in one of His creations, it will rise to the surface despite the soil. I grew up in a very undesirable, neglectful environment. But like Zach, I skipped grades and was also a National Merit Scholarship finalist.

Then, too, the thing is not to get hung up on intelligence as the most important gift. I have other children who are gifted singers or extraordinary parents or just plain wonderful human beings, full of kindness and character.

Mommies, this is what it's all about. As Rick Warren's *The Purpose-Driven Life* begins—"It's not about you."

I couldn't agree more! It's not about us—it's all about them. It's all about receiving each one as though God has given us a very special gift, not planning who or what they will become but unwrapping carefully to see what God has placed inside, then doing our best to help them realize their potential.

 FUN STUFF

Toads-in-a-Hole

While we're on the subject of Zachary, his specialty recipe is Toads-in-a-Hole. He started making them when he was a little boy. This is something you can teach a six-year-old who is able to concentrate and be careful at the stove.

Use a small glass or biscuit cutter to cut a hole in the center of a piece of bread. Melt butter on griddle, and place bread on melted butter. Add a little more butter in the circle. Crack and drop an egg into center. Flip when done on one side. When egg is just right for you, remove from griddle. Enjoy!

I don't know which part of Toads-in-a-Hole Zachary liked most—the making, the eating, or maybe the name. But your kids will probably like them for all the same reasons.

 HERE'S HELP

How to Handle a Stutter—and Come to Think of It, Lots of Other Stuff

No child's speech develops perfectly smoothly. Twenty-five percent go through a stage of disfluency severe enough to worry their parents. But only one percent end up as permanent stutterers (four times as many boys as girls).

The best approach is to wait and see if a stutter resolves on its own. If your child gets stuck on sounds or words, just be patient, and wait for him to finish what he is saying. Don't prompt your child to re-lax, slow down, or start over. Don't finish words or sentences. Simply relax yourself, maintain eye contact, and look interested in what he is saying. Respond just as you would have responded had his fluency been perfect.

Train other family members, friends, and babysitters to respond in the same way. It's important for the child not to become tense or alarmed about speech, because that can prolong the problem—perhaps even contributing to a permanent stutter.

How will you know when your child has a serious problem? The Stuttering Foundation of America (hotline number 901-992-9392, web site <http://www.stuttersfa.org>) offers a wealth of information, comfort, and advice for concerned families, friends, and teachers.

For a stutter that persists for a few months, you might want to check with a speech therapist who's trained to recognize a potential stuttering problem and work out an appropriate program of treatment.

Before drawing extra attention to the stutter—or any other problem for that matter—try praying and seeing if you can just watch it come to pass.

Kids will be kids—let them.

DIGGING HOLES

SIX

Yikes! What is it with kids and dirt? The afternoon I discovered our kids had been digging ditches in our back yard, I started, like any mother, to react in typical fashion: I told them to stop—now, immediately, forever.

But before I could speak (or scream), they spotted me. And an impromptu celebration began.

"Mommy, Mommy, c'mere!"

"Look at all this work we've done!"

"I did this one all by myself!"

"We're going to do more and then play soldiers!"

Breathing a silent *Thank You* that I had been given a reprieve from raining on their parade, I mustered up all the admiration I could for their morning's work.

And the most amazing thing of all? I wasn't insincere. Because beyond my initial shock, beyond the upheaval of dirt and grass, I had caught a glimpse of something transcendent on my children's faces—like the look we adults get when we've finished building a bridge or writing a novel or filling a cavity, that incredible satisfaction that comes when we know we've set out and accomplished something truly worthwhile. And so instead of destruction, my mommy eyes could see that for children, digging ditches could be as constructive and worthwhile as anything I could have dreamed up for them to do.

First of all, they had come up with a project on their own. They worked together as a team. Brothers and sisters, older and younger—all shoveled and spaded and hoed in harmony. As individuals, each had concentrated on a task for a few hours. Television, videos, computer games—all were forgotten as their focus was fixed on meeting a goal. They had worked hard, and they were proud of it.

This is the kind of character-building mommies dream of!

One of the wonderful things I've discovered as a mom who depends on the Holy Spirit is that because of that dependence, I'm free—free to see things fresh and new each day, free not to blindly repeat the patterns of the past, free not to react the way my mother might have, even free not to react the way I once might have myself.

Being a mommy involves on-the-job training. You just have to be open at all times to the lessons coming your way. The more open you are to them, the more quickly you'll learn. The more quickly you learn, the more job satisfaction you'll find and the more confidence you'll have that *Yes, I can do this job well and have fun at it too!*

So while we may not get the bonuses or trophies, we can have the satisfaction of knowing that when we do something the right way—as when I refrained from murdering two-year-old Ben when he brought a hose into the house and watered our green carpet (yes, "murdering" is a strong word, but you know what I mean)—we can feel the pleasure of our Heavenly Father as He watches over His children. And don't forget: we're His children just as they are. And He forgives our messes and mistakes—especially when we don't know any better—because He knows we're on a learning curve.

Why not go as gently with them as He goes with us? Why not be as patient and generous and quick to forgive? These will be the very qualities that will shape their perception of God in the years ahead. And so even as we try to help our kids reach their potential, God is at work helping us reach ours.

Our kids are like lesson plans: *Everything I know about being a mom, I learned while my kids were digging ditches/watering the carpet/putting dirty clothes into the dryer . . .*

This one's pretty simple:

- Certain things kids need to accomplish have nothing to do with the work at hand but the character that's being built while they're busy.
- Mommies need to remember to think outside the box. And don't forget to breathe.
- You can appreciate the ditches, but it's OK to limit them to one part of the yard so as to maintain your sanity and good relations with your neighbors

 FUN STUFF

Dirt Cake

2 pkgs. (20 oz. each) Oreo cookies
½ stick butter
8 oz. cream cheese

1 c. powdered sugar
3½ c. milk
2 small boxes French vanilla instant pudding
1 (12 oz.) Cool Whip

Cream butter, cream cheese, and powdered sugar.
Mix pudding with the milk; add Cool Whip.
Blend cream cheese and pudding mixtures.
Crumble the Oreos in a blender.

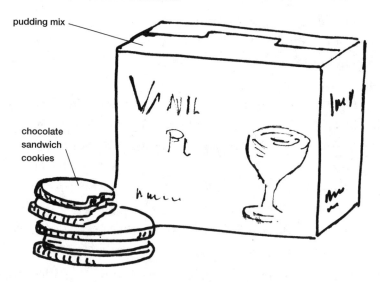

pudding mix

chocolate
sandwich
cookies

Line the inside of a brand new clay flower pot with foil. Alternate
cookie crumbs and filling, ending with the cookie crumbs on top. Top
with artificial flowers and gummy worms. Serve with a new garden
trowel.

Enjoy!

Movie Date

Holes (2003, Disney, PG) is all about digging—and other fascinating
stuff. An exciting and faithful adaptation of the book by Louis Sachar,
it's a movie the whole family will enjoy, filled with down-to-earth kids
and vivid adult characters (Sigourney Weaver, John Voight).

NEW-BABY BLUES

SEVEN

I get some of my best material from readers' questions. The following is one I recently received—a variation on the theme of sibling rivalry (which I'll be talking about more in the chapter "Get a Grip on Sibling Rivalry"). And while the writer is talking about a "tween" (the trendy name for kids on the verge of becoming teens), the principles apply to all children.

Like it or not, the birth of a baby can produce post-partum stress in other members of the family besides Mom. I know it's hard when you're overwhelmed with your own baby blues. I'll never forget the times I burst into tears in the middle of dinner, to the great distress of my family. But besides losing sleep and grappling with your own changing emotional landscape, you have to do your best to help your kids deal with theirs.

Just don't forget: it comes to pass, not to stay!

Here's the question:

On October 31 I welcomed our fourth child. Yea! He is an absolute joy. However, as with each baby, there is always that adjustment period, which I always find so hard. My oldest seems to have the hardest time adjusting. She is 12, and I also have a 4-year-old and a 3-year-old. So there is a big space between my oldest daughter and my other children.

I know you can relate to this with your two girls being older than your other children. Often I feel she is left out, and at this preteen stage, she *does* need my attention. I find she is actually the hardest one, because she needs to talk, and I need to focus to listen, and she is easy to overlook because she does so much for herself. I find it hard to change gears with her emotional needs and then the physical needs of the younger ones. It's hard.

I am feeling overwhelmed with everyone's needs. Through experience I know that this will even out and we all will adjust, but I am finding that my oldest gives me the most worry and the most challenges in care.

I hope you know what I am saying. Mostly I am just writing to you to see if you experienced this with your two older girls and what you did. I need practical advice as well as encouragement.

My reply:

When Josh was born, Samantha was 14 and Jasmine 7. Samantha was pretty secure and adjusted well—although when we announced nine months later that we were going to have another baby, she fled the dinner table in tears. But Jasmine had been the baby for almost eight years, and she had very mixed feelings.

With a stream of visitors coming to meet the new baby, Jasmine reacted to her perceived dethroning by staging elaborate puppet shows and raffles for our guests. A little over-the-top, but at least it was a constructive way to handle those feelings of jealousy.

But Jasmine wasn't in denial about her feelings, and she actually was able to laugh at her own coping mechanisms. She was the one who came up with the term *shooganoona* to describe those times when she would hug the baby just a little too tightly, squeeze his cheek a little too hard.

It was a word to describe that sibling ambivalence —*I love this baby, but I don't love how he's taking my parents away from me. I want to play with him, but I want to hurt him too.* That word—*shooganoona*—was a blessing, because it gave a name to something we didn't have a name for. It made it possible to discuss the feelings and laugh about how crazy they can make us. It helped defuse them, so in the end there were fewer *shooganoonas* in the house.

While your oldest is probably beyond *shooganoonas*, she may have the same ambivalent feelings. You can never predict for sure who will be hit the hardest by each new birth. But when you see it, you need to give that child a little extra.

At 12, a girl is very much in need of quality time from Dad and from Mom. How about Dad taking her out to breakfast (that was always a big thrill for our kids), taking her shopping with you when you might have gone alone, going to see a movie, or browsing through art books at the library? Set aside an hour to go through old family photo albums and talk about her. Or if you have family videos, you could watch them together while you nurse the baby, and focus the conversation on your daughter. You could give her some extra high-status responsibilities and privileges—something not connected to the baby.

Also, she's old enough to talk with frankly about her feelings, which she may not have even consciously sorted through herself. You can approach it in a safe, indirect way by asking her how she thinks the younger kids have adjusted and what kind of difference the baby has made in the house, what she misses most, what she likes the most. You might even start a conversation by telling her about this family you know whose daughter thought up the word *shooganoona*—and what it meant.

HERE'S HELP

For reasons I'll go into in an upcoming chapter, "Say It with Stories," when it comes to dealing with kids' emotional quandaries, books with animal characters can teach important lessons in charming and nonthreatening ways. In *A Baby Sister for Frances*, the whimsical badgerette takes to sitting under the kitchen sink, singing her usual random songs and blaming the baby for the all the disruption in the household routine and the fact that her parents don't seem to notice her as they used to.

When a new baby comes home, another child in the family may experience mixed emotions. He loves the new baby, but mixed with the love and natural tenderness toward a smaller, more vulnerable being are feelings of jealousy and anger for which the child has no name. These feelings are frightening and confusing:

Mommy says I'm good when I'm nice to the baby. But when he cries, I want to smoosh him under the pillow. I must be very bad.

At this age, a child needs you to help him or her develop the communication tools needed to keep emotions from controlling behavior. So start with Frances, who looks different on the outside but seems to be struggling with the same feeling.

In the book, when Frances's parents grab the chance to reassure her, their child's anxiety is relieved. Reading her story gives you a chance to reassure your own child and—if the time seems right—to go on to talk about the issue closer to home. How does she feel about the new baby? What can she do when she feels left out and blue? *Why, come and tell Mommy or Daddy you need a hug too!*

 FUN STUFF

No matter how young or old your displaced child, he or she will enjoy spending time with you in the kitchen making something special that the baby is too young to enjoy.

Peanut Butter Balls

2 c. peanut butter
1 c. nonfat dry milk
¼ c. honey
1½ c. peanuts, coconut, raisins, sunflower seeds, raisins, or any combination
1 c. crushed granola or sesame seeds

Mix first four ingredients together in bowl. Roll into small balls. Roll in crushed granola or sesame seeds, then place on wax paper. Refrigerate until firm.

One of the ways to get your displaced child feeling more secure is to give him or her some new skills to feel more grown-up about. Now might be a good time to develop some cooking skills: try *The Everything Kids' Cookbook* (Adams Media Corp.) for a good kid-friendly introduction. Add a few sighs like "I'm glad we have someone in the family old enough to cook!" and watch your child shine.

KEEPING KIDS BUSY
EIGHT

This question follows fast on the heels of the last:

When they were all little, how do you or did you find time to properly care for and supervise your children and get your housework done? I really struggle with this one. It is either one or the other. If I have all my children with me, I get nothing done. If I send them outside unsupervised, before I know it they are yelling and fighting among themselves. Could you please be honest and tell me how you managed when your children were all little?

My reply:

There are two parts to this answer. The first has to do with learning to work with your children so you'll have time to play. The second involves preparing your home to give them opportunities to amuse themselves independently.

First of all, it's truly amazing with each additional child how much less important housework becomes. I only wish I had relaxed more about housework with my first children. I'm in my fifties now with six children still at home (my youngest by birth is 12, but the last three are adopted, and they're 10, 9, and 5), and I'm definitely s-l-o-w-i-n-g down.

To tell you the truth, there are days I don't get around to making our bed (it's upstairs and easy to avoid). I figure that when I'm on my deathbed and my kids are gathered around, no one is going to *tch, tch* and remember all the days that Mommy didn't make her bed. Most of you moms reading this are probably younger and not writing about your motherhood experience (yet), so you probably still should be making your beds. But I'm an older mom, and slowing down is forcing a choice. I have to believe that the time I put into my kids is just more worthwhile. While it took me many years of motherhood to really get this straight, if you can grab onto it sooner, you'll be better off than I was.

You need to involve your children in helping around the house before they're out of diapers so that the family ethic becomes one of a team taking responsibility for and working together to keep the house in good shape so that everyone enjoys it. Even when you're young and energetic enough to do it all, you have to let go, because it will make your life easier later on, and it's essential in unlocking the goodness in your children.

What works best for me is to fully dedicate some time to my kids and then expect some time of independent play. Go outside and run around with them, blow bubbles, fly a kite, read a book together—anything in which you're totally involved. Then say, "Now it's time for Mommy to do some work of her own [or read a book or whatever]. What will *you* do?" If your children are younger, help them decide. Set a timer, or show them a clock for whatever length of time you need or they can handle.

The second part of empowering your children to spend time on their own involves creating lots of opportunities in the environment.

Let's start with babies.

My experience is that babies like to spend time in high chairs—probably because they're more at our level. I took advantage of that by following a meal with the current baby just sitting in the high chair while the rest of us cleaned the kitchen. Give the baby Cheerios (which have the double advantage of keeping the baby busy while perfecting pincer grasp—which eventually leads to handwriting skills) or a spoonful of peanut butter (if there are no allergies) to dip little fingers in. These activities may occupy a lot of time. When the snack is gone, wash the baby's face, and give her a clean, damp washcloth to practice washing her own face and to fool around with, and then maybe a toy to play with.

Keep your Tupperware, measuring cups, pots, pans, and lids in lower cabinets where your children can play with them. This may sound crazy to first-time mothers or fastidious types, but you can always wipe something out before you use it, and you're guaranteeing much happiness to your child. Just be sure to teach the child to put them away!

Have you noticed that the things toddlers like to play with are usually things that Mom and Dad use? Examples: a toy vacuum, child-sized broom and dustpan, feather duster. Take those fake credit cards that come in the mail, and put them into an old wallet. Put pictures in too. Put the wallet into an old purse. Put in a lip balm stick, a ring of useless old keys, a handkerchief, and so on. You can add new things as you think of them and hang it on a certain door knob. This will become a "work" station—because the play of a toddler is really *work*. It's what the toddler was built to do—to stay busy. Our job is simply to try to stay a little ahead of the game.

How about a rack of dress-up clothes—suit jacket, hats, a feather boa, beads, scarves, fancy shoes? Also include a mirror at their height so your children can enjoy the costumes they put together.

I've mentioned a child-sized table. Have a shelf next to it with puzzles and coloring books and other activities. Make sure you have enough seats for all your children, and encourage them to do some things sitting at the table. You might set out a basket of shells or stones or large decorative buttons just to look at— maybe with a magnifying glass.

Make sure your children's books are gathered neatly on a shelf or board books are in a basket. It's nice to have a child's chair or beanbag nearby. Teach the children to pick out a book, take it to a chair, and read it.

If your children are not reliable with books, use board books until they can be trusted.

Think in terms of creating spaces within your environment that become places that invite your children to settle down and do something they enjoy.

Honestly, in my experience I have not had a lot of kids yelling and fighting with each other (other than teenage girls sniping). I believe that the more we understand our children and try to meet their basic needs for independence, order, and learning to serve, the less negative behavior we see.

I do hear what you're saying. These beginning years of motherhood are very demanding and very difficult. It takes a lot of faith to think you'll ever make it through. But if you train your children well, by the time they're six or seven years old, they can be major helpers, and then you'll begin to come out of that stage and into the next stage of motherhood, which is still very busy but definitely easier.

Still, every day is a balancing act.

The more tools you have, the better—so do try to carve out a little time each day to improve your motherhood skills. Each new thing you learn will help. Sometimes it will feel as though you're taking two steps forward and one step back. That's OK. Someday, looking back, you'll wonder how it all went by so fast.

And through it all, just remember how pleased and delighted God must be that you're doing this wonderful work to see to the needs of His children.

MOMMY POWER

First We/Then We

One of the best lessons your child can learn is delayed gratification. You can start very early and easily to teach this by simply setting up things in a sequential fashion with work first and entertainment later. It sounds like this:

"First we clean up the kitchen and fold the laundry—then we can play outside."

"First we put away all the toys—then we can watch a DVD."

"First we finish our school work—then we can go shopping."

"First we do all our chores—then we leave for the movies."

Notice how much more positive this sounds than "If you don't do your chores we won't go to the movies." I promise you—it will get a better response!

Lists

When your children are older, try making a checklist of chores. I keep a master list on my computer so I can select whatever needs to be done—along with spaces for check marks.

I find my kids grab the list with enthusiasm and divide the chores and get things done very quickly. In fact, when one is old enough to baby-sit, I've found they do the best job if I leave the list and go shopping. Voilà! I come home, and everything's done without the need to nag.

Inspiration

Children are a poor man's riches.
—English proverb

The soul is healed by being with children.
—Fyodor Dostoyevski

Children are the hands by which we take hold of heaven.
—Henry Ward Beecher

We find delight in the beauty and happiness of children that makes the heart too big for the body.
—Ralph Waldo Emerson, *The Conduct of Life*

We can't form our children on our own concepts; we must take them and love them as God gives them to us.
—Johann Wolfgang von Goethe

Lo, children are an heritage of the LORD: and the fruit of the womb is his reward.
—Ps. 127:3 (KJV)

IT'S OK TO WIN OR LOSE

NINE

We have four boys in a row, which can make for some dramatic competitive moments, especially when they're several hours into a "Risk!" game and the youngest—whose name I will not mention here—goes bananas and pounds the table and sweeps the board and all armies off the table and onto the floor, causing much outrage and gnashing of teeth among his older brothers.

Some people are more competitive than others. Some people should wear a warning sign: "Stay Out of My Way!" Some people just have a little more growing-up to do.

Nowadays mommies tend to worry too much about competition. That's because competition has been given a bad rap by people who care mostly about making sure everyone feels good. From scoreless soccer games to only pass-or-fail grading in school to trophies being given to all team players and not just to the stars, this cultural trend has gone way overboard. So when competitiveness crops up in siblings, a mommy may overreact as well, trying to nip this "negative" behavior in the bud.

But is competition really negative? Not when you consider that our culture's achievements, improvements, and inventions are brought about by individuals with the strong drive to succeed. This energy, which manifests as competition, is vital.

What does this mean for mommies? It means that rather than squashing kids' competitiveness, we need to—

- differentiate between healthy and unhealthy competition, and
- provide opportunities to channel the competitive spirit in ways that will build up our children rather than tear them down.

First of all, you have to know your kids.

From the earliest years, you should be on the lookout for special gifts and talents in your kids so you can reinforce and help strengthen them. For instance, a musically mediocre mommy may find that her son is interested in opera. She can sign him up for chorus, check out opera CDs from the library, maybe even find some local operas to attend together. (This really happened in our family, and now that almost grown-up son is studying opera at the university.) A father who played only baseball may learn to coach soccer just to give his daughter with promise a boost.

Following our children's leads in developing their talents keeps us from forcing them all into the same mold. There's no reason why all the children in the family should take piano, and one good reason why they shouldn't: if each child plays a different instrument, there will be less room for competition, more room for harmonious undertakings.

Keeping in mind that competition is basically healthful, be on the lookout for times when it's not. When competition turns to rivalry, when hostility is involved—as when kids are competing to gain parental approval—parents do have a problem.

Here are some suggestions for defusing volatile relationships when competition has gotten out of hand:

- **Avoid favoritism and comparisons**. Avoid lavishing attention on the ones who succeed at the expense of those who may be falling behind. Using God's unconditional love as your example, let children know you love them for who they are—and that you love their brothers and sisters that way too.

- **Make sure each child has one-on-one time with Mom and Dad**. Dad may make a ritual of taking one child to breakfast each Saturday. Mom may make a practice of taking just one to help with grocery shopping. Make sure no one gets overlooked.

- **Provide opportunities for lots of talk around the issue**. If one child is very competitive, another may give up completely. Neither position is healthy. A parent's job is then to encourage the withdrawn child not to give up, to teach the assertive one to be more sensitive to others.

- **Know where to draw the line between healthful competition and rivalry**. When brothers play "Risk!" for example, and things get out of hand, sore players should be removed from the game and given a "cool down" time.

- **Create a balance by building a sense of team spirit into your family life**. Adopt a family motto—something like The Three Musketeers' "One for all and all for one!"—or make a family banner with symbols of the qualities that make your family unique.

As in so many other areas of bringing up our kids, we must be alert to keeping things in perspective. Just keep in mind that healthful competition is a good thing and can bring out the best in everyone. Don't go overboard in reining it in.

 HERE'S HELP

If competition is getting out of hand, put away video and board games for a while. Instead, try a 500- or 1,000-piece jigsaw puzzle that you can work on together in snatches until it's finished. Or work together on creating a family banner with symbols of all the things that mean a lot to your family.

Nothing beats a family service project—serving meals to the homeless, visiting a nursing home, stuffing envelopes for a rescue mission. Instead of just Mom or Dad or kids in the youth group getting involved, do it as a family.

Movie Date

Chariots of Fire (1981, Warner Brothers, PG) contrasts the competitive spirit between two athletes—one who places his faith in himself and one who places his faith in God. Eric Liddel's remark "God made me fast, and when I run I feel His pleasure" will resonate with anyone who is following a divine plan—including mommies! *God gave me children, and when I mother I feel His pleasure.*

Our job as mommies includes waiting for God to reveal His purpose in each of our children's lives so they may find that special niche and someday say, "When I _____, I feel God's pleasure."

THE TRUTH ABOUT BOYS AND GIRLS

TEN

Snakes and snails and puppy dog tails? Sugar and spice and everything nice?

What are little boys and girls made of after all? Before the 1960s, this question sparked little controversy. You had a daughter, you raised a girl. You had a son, you raised a boy. But then along came the feminist movement, poking holes in all our preconceived notions of "girlness" and "boyness." "We need to raise boys the way we raise girls," said Gloria Steinem—thus blessing "girl" behavior as the norm and boy behavior as aberrant.

Parents and educators became persuaded that differences in behavior between girls and boys are not inborn but a result of the way they're raised.

But are they?

As a former teacher and now a megamommy, I've been riding the nature-versus-nurture pendulum for years. In fact, I gave it a good push myself, prompted by the birth of my daughter Samantha in 1969. My feminist period began with our first trip to the library, where I noted with alarm the absence of girls in kids' books (thankfully, this has changed). Ever the conscientious mother, I spent hours replacing pronouns and feminizing male critters of every species (think curled and beribboned bird in *Are You My Mother?*). I firmly believed that boys and girls were different only because of parental programming. Fourteen years later, I had to admit I was wrong, not because anyone persuaded me but because I ran into evidence I couldn't dispute.

I gave birth to a son.

The moment nine-month-old Josh scooted his spoon across his high chair tray making engine noises, I met my feminist Waterloo. When he purposely ran headlong into danger, wrestled with his sisters' dolls, and sidestepped my domestic disarmament policy by turning every stick and sausage link into a gun, I had to concede that there must be something to this innate difference thing.

Recognize the reality of gender differences. After years of assuming gender differences are more about societal programming, science has now confirmed what our grandmothers never stopped believing: Boys and girls are different.

Even as infants, boys have higher levels of testosterone, which stimulates aggressive behavior, and lower levels of serotonin, which inhibits it. Researchers have found that infant boys cry more when unhappy while girls tend to comfort themselves by sucking their thumbs. Even at this early stage, girls seem to have more control of their emotions.

Newborn girls spend more time than newborn boys maintaining eye contact with adults. At four months, infant girls have better face recognition than boys. Conversely, infant boys are better able to track a blinking light across a television monitor (a portent of adolescent video fixation?) and will gaze as intently at a blinking light as at a human face.

Flash forward four years. Now the differences are even greater, with girls better equipped for building relationships and interpreting emotions and boys gifted with a better understanding of spatial relationships—knowledge greatly in demand in complex societies.

Then there are the differences in language. A friend of mine—mother of four girls in a row, then two boys—described her experience this way: "The most noticeable difference has to be the vehicle-noise-imitation thing. In 11 years I never once heard the girls make any noise that sounded like a vehicle revving up. But when Sawyer was 12 months old, he picked up a toy airplane and "flew" it complete with airplane sounds. At the same age, Kellen did the same thing with a motorcycle."

You mothers of boys know what I'm talking about!

In fact, researchers found boys use words only 60 percent of the time and a variety of colorful noises the remainder of the time, while girls use words almost exclusively—as anyone who takes kids to the playground knows.

Genetically, each child is a unique package of possibilities. Certain predispositions will be expressed if environmental conditions are right. And these may fade or flourish depending on how they're reinforced. Stanley Greenspan, pediatric psychiatrist at George Washington University and author of The Growth of the Mind (Perseus Books), compares the relationship between genetics and environment to a Fred Astaire/Ginger Rogers dance. "If either Fred or Ginger moves too fast, they both stumble. Nature affects nurture affects nature and back and forth. Each step influences the next."

So even as science keeps changing its mind, it's clear to parents everywhere that boys and girls truly are different creatures from the moment they arrive. It's what we do with those differences that matters.

Let boys and girls express their innate differences. Those unconvinced about gender differences need to check out school recess, where boy-girl differences show up in the middle-class suburbs and tough inner-city schools, crossing all racial and economic lines. Girls tend to hang out in groups of two or three, in intimate discussion. They make eye contact, listen intently, and work at building relationships. As often as not, it's relationships they're discussing with parents, teachers, siblings, other friends. They choose games like hopscotch and jump rope, in which everyone gets a turn. Differences in skills are minimized, and the atmosphere is supportive. Girls want to be liked.

Boys, on the other hand, freshly sprung from the enforced immobility of the classroom, are often raucous, rowdy, and rambunctious. They play in large groups, in a constant struggle for one-upmanship that serves to reveal the leader of the pack. Their games are structured, complex, and focused on scores. Boys want to win.

And that can present a problem. Nowadays, many educators regard the normal play of boys with disapproval.

Picking up on the Steinem theme, they've structured the school day with no regard for boys' natural patterns of activity, attitudes, and behavior. Some schools, ignoring boys' need for decompression time, have even scrapped free-play recess for more structured activities with no competition.

Competition is out in the classroom as well. Games with winners—even musical chairs—have been replaced by more cooperative activities. If that sounds good to you, it's because you're a woman. Studies consistently show boys do better in competitive environments, so the competition-free atmosphere of some classrooms can actually cause them to become frustrated and aggressive.

Despite past research to the contrary, newer studies have found that today's elementary classrooms are more geared to the success of girls than that of boys. Coming into kindergarten, boys are more immature: besides needing plenty of gross motor activity, they learn to read later, and their fine motor skills (such as finger grasp for writing) usually lag behind those of girls. One way to compensate is to have boys start school a year later—an option many parents choose.

Some "experts" read the active, more assertive behavior of boys as indicating a propensity to violence. But this line of thinking shows a lack of respect for the unique qualities God has built into boys—the qualities that will someday make them men.

For mothers, it's often difficult to understand our sons' need for physical and aggressive play. With eight sons, I know. I've done a lot of biting my tongue as I watched them roughhouse and wrestle. But I've learned to respect the fact that they are who they are and that they need to express themselves without constant interference from women.

The truth is, we need to respect the right of girls to be girls and boys to be boys. Some experts push for "integrated" play between boys and girls, though many studies show children between kindergarten and sixth grade prefer same-sex play. Our kids aren't sexless. They have distinct needs and preferences. We owe it to them to let them be who God created them to be.

Mostly, we need to relax and enjoy our kids as individuals. Most parents realize that the differences between boys and girls are far from absolute. Each boy is somewhere on a continuum of maleness and each girl on a continuum of femaleness. There is certainly crossover. Some boys are more relationship-oriented than some girls, some girls more competitive than some boys.

The best approach is to be on the lookout for ways to encourage your child's unique gifts and personality, regardless of gender. If that means signing your son up for tap dancing lessons or helping your daughter build a tree fort, do it.

Most important, look for the godly character traits behind your child's interests. A boy who prefers dolls to trucks probably has a strong nurturing side, a fantastic quality in any child. A girl who's a strong leader on the soccer field probably has the self-confidence to influence her peers in other positive ways.

Even if the scientific community changes its tune to-

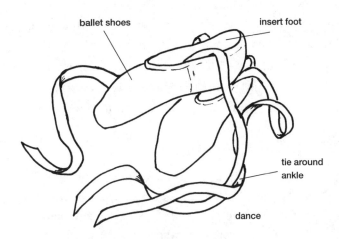

Boys like to dance, too, and I wouldn't want to hinder a budding male ballet dancer, but their taste usually runs to Sousa pieces for marching and maybe a little "William Tell Overture."

But both agree on '50s music. When you need a little pickup at home, put on some golden oldies like "At the Hop," "Rockin' Robin," "A Whole Lotta Shakin' Goin' On." Those old hits are bound to keep everyone happy.

As far as kids' music, my favorites are *Baby Face*—a cute collection of songs with "baby" in the title that's designed to encourage interactive musical moments for Mom and baby or toddler. I started singing one of these songs the other day, and my oldest son, 22-year-old Josh, pricked up his ears, got a misty look in his eyes, and started singing along too. Happy memories!

Raffi's Singable Songs is a three-disc collection worth every penny. I've been singing these songs along with my kids for 22 years, which indicates they're a cut above most kids' music. I would say that what C. S. Lewis said of books—"It certainly is my opinion that a book worth reading only in childhood is not worth reading even then"—must be true of music as well. Anything by Raffi is guaranteed to please kids.

Deep in the Jungle is by Joe Scruggs. Ditto what I said about Raffi. But Joe Scruggs isn't just warm. He's witty and always fresh and fun. Best of all, he appeals to all ages from toddler to adult.

morrow, the essential truth in the gender discussion is this: God created us to complement and complete each other as males and females. Wherever your child is on the male-female continuum, you can delight in knowing that his or her placement is part of God's perfect plan.

MOMMY POWER

Things You Need to Know

- Elementary-age boys and girls typically prefer same-sex play. If your child wants to play with the opposite sex, that's great, but don't push him or her into unwanted relationships.
- Boys thrive on competition, girls on cooperative activities. If you insist that your child deny these natural tendencies, it will likely frustrate him or her. Give your child opportunities to play both competitive and noncompetitive games.
- Male behavior is no better or worse than female behavior. It's just different. Do your best to accept your son as he is. While you don't want to encourage dangerous or disrespectful behavior, remember that being rambunctious or loud isn't necessarily bad behavior. Help your son find appropriate outlets for his energy.
- Teachers who don't respect boys for who they are can be harmful. Make sure your son's teacher has reasonable expectations for all the students. Most of all, check in with your son to assess his feelings about his teacher. If you sense a problem, talk with the teacher and work together to find ways to help your son get the most from his class.

 FUN STUFF

Music and Dance!

Even if she's not in dance glass, your little girl will love being a ballerina. Get her a ballerina outfit of some kind and some classical music to dance to, such as *Swan Lake* or *Sleeping Beauty*.

A little bit of Mommy goes a long way.

SAY IT WITH STORIES

ELEVEN

In the great green room there was a telephone and a red balloon and a cow jumping over the moon.

To this day my oldest son, now 22, gets a googly-eyed smile when he hears his mommy read these lines, though these days I'm reading to the younger brothers still at home. That goes to show how the stories we read our children night after night stay nestled in their hearts forever.

I know they've nestled in mine. Thirty-six years of turning pages with my children hasn't diminished at all the wonder of children's stories. I still perk up at the rhythms and the well-chosen words of "Brown Bear, Brown Bear, What Do You See?" I'm still captivated by the whimsical images of "Runaway Bunny."

But there's much more in those pages than meets the ear and eye. And the longer I read with my kids, books like *The Rainbow Fish* and *Where the Wild Things Are* and *The Chronicles of Narnia* and *David Copperfield*, the more I appreciate the deeper impact stories have on the lives of children.

Stories give meaning and structure to the way a child sees the world. They offer a safe context for sorting out feelings. They define the child's placement in the world and lead to a feeling of security.

How do they do all that? That's a good thing to learn, for when you understand how stories work, you'll be able to pick those that have the most positive impact on your children's character and will help you help them over the bumps on the growing-up journey.

Kinds of Stories

Though adults know the difference between reality and fantasy, young children do not. Unless we help them sort it out, they're likely to assume David and Goliath live in the same part of the world as Jack and the Beanstalk.

While books are usually divided into the two categories of fiction and nonfiction, with children's stories it's more helpful to think in terms of three:

- Stories that really happened
  Historical events or figures
  Bible stories
- Stories that could happen
  Fictional characters facing real dilemmas, such as *Ira Sleeps Over, A Chair for My Mother*
- Stories that could never happen at all
  Animal characters or fantastic situations, such as *Little Red Riding Hood, Bedtime for Frances*

Each type of story has a special contribution to make in the development of the child.

What Really Happened

As someone wise once said, "He who has the best story wins."

Maybe that's why God gave us the Bible, because it's the very best story of all, from creation through the fall of humanity from God's grace to the stunning tale of our redemption.

Then there are the subplots, hundreds of colorful, compelling stories: an ark, a baby in a basket, a baby in a manger, blind men who see, baskets of loaves and fishes. As someone who grew up without the Bible, I found these stories absolutely thrilling when I read them for the first time with my children in *The Bible in Picture for Little Eyes* and *Read-Aloud Bible Stories*.

And how much more because I knew they were true! Since these stories are the foundation of our faith, be sure your children understand that they're different from lots of other stories they'll read—because they really happened.

Ditto for biographies and books of other cultures. If it's something your child hasn't seen firsthand, don't forget to state clearly that it was or is real—that if your child lived in a different time or place, he or she would be able to see these things firsthand.

What Could Happen

How exciting to be invited to spend the night at a friend's house, but how scary the prospect of having him find out you still sleep with your teddy bear! In *Ira Sleeps Over*, this typical seven-year-old crisis is handled with empathy and humor.

How terrible to lose your home and belongings in a fire, but how wonderful to have a mother who works hard as a waitress to earn the family's daily bread! She deserves a special reward, a place to relax when she comes home. In *A Chair for My Mother,* she gets it.

In *Where's Our Mama?* a mother's hat blows away in a train station, and she leaves her three children to chase it. The three enlist help to find their mother, but their clues—Mama is the best cook, has the best voice, is the bravest—lead them all over Paris to a chef, opera singer, and lion tamer. Only when they remember Mama said to stay put do they return to find her waiting.

Stories that address the fears and problems of childhood one-step-removed play a special role in children's reading. By "one-step-removed," I mean stories told by or about a child with whom the reader can consciously identify. These stories bring issues to the surface, spark discussion, promise resolution, offer hope and reassurance.

What Couldn't Happen at All

Not everyone agrees on the role of fantasy in children's reading. Some parents and educators are adamant that children should read only books that are reality-based.

For instance, Maria Montessori believed that since young children could not think abstractly—could not distinguish between fantasy and reality—introducing fantasy into their lives would only confuse them. Besides, she reasoned, reality is so full of marvelous things that we can easily fill the early years just teaching children all the wonders of the world, saving fantasy for later.

Likewise, some parents, because of their spiritual convictions, wish to avoid fantasy or even stories that have animals as talking characters.

I see great value in fantasy, although it requires a little extra discernment on the part of parents to make sure that the author's agenda—because every author has one—is compatible with what they want their children to learn.

Books with animal characters—I especially think of Russell Hoban's Frances books—can teach important lessons in charming and nonthreatening ways. In *A Baby Sister for Frances*, the whimsical badgerette deals with sibling rivalry. *A Birthday for Frances* deals with the ebb and tide of generosity and jealousy when it's someone else's birthday. *Bedtime for Frances* deals with the fears of going to bed. *Bread and Jam for Frances* deals with the parent-child struggle over eating the right foods.

All these typical childhood problems could be dealt with in a once-removed setting with a real child like Ira. But they wouldn't pack the wallop they do here.

That's because these books address something scarier than being lost, poverty, or embarrassment. They address the child's fear of his or her own emotions.

Though sibling rivalry and anger toward parents are normal, the child doesn't know that, and when these feelings well up, they're ugly and frightening. *Mommy says I'm good when I'm nice to the baby. But when he cries, I want to smoosh him under the pillow. I must be very bad.*

Unlike adults who can reason through emotional conflicts when we feel something we would rather not, children lack the language and tools. What works for them are stories twice-removed, like the Frances books, in which the unreasonable feelings are projected onto a creature that doesn't look like the child on the outside but seems a lot like him or her on the inside. That Frances is transparent, that she warbles funny tunes about her quandaries, and that her parents love her no matter what—these make the stories even more appealing and fill the child with hope.

So use discernment. But don't forget that there's more to stories than meets the eye. Make room for books that help your children with their dilemmas today. Then rejoice when you find them still nestled in their hearts tomorrow.

 ## MAKING CHANGES

A Reader-Friendly Environment

Tripp and I love books, and there have always been plenty around. It took only a little effort to teach our kids to respect books, and we've been able to keep lovely art books on the coffee table for browsing by the older kids.

For your younger ones, create a reading nook with a beanbag or cozy little chair next to a shelf of their own books. Make sure the light is good, and decorate with any pictures you can find of people—especially children—reading.

 ## HERE'S HELP!

Want to begin building a library for your children? It may be easier and less expensive than you think!

Check secondhand stores and garage sales for used books, and make sure they're in good repair before buying them. If you bring books with torn or drawn-on pages into your home, it will give your child the idea that it's OK to do these things to books. If you want your child to respect books, they must be in good condition.

Let grandparents, friends, and family know that you would love to receive books for baby gifts. If you have several children and they receive books for gifts, you'll build a respectable library faster than you think.

And books are better anyway. Trust me—a good book will hold your child's attention much longer than most toys, and books have the advantage of no missing pieces, and they don't clutter your house as much. Books also have a longer lifespan than toys. Books have a way of growing up with a child. I've heard of college-bound teens who've asked their parents not to get rid of their own childhood libraries. They want them for their own children.

One of my daughter Samantha's favorite books when she was growing up was *Jellybeans for Breakfast*. Long out of print, it now fetches up to $175 on Ebay or Amazon Used Books from 30-something women who remember it fondly and want to read it to their daughters.

RAISING KIDS WITH SELF-CONTROL

TWELVE

One of the greatest gifts you can give your child is self-control. It's not the kind of gift you can wrap a bow around but a foundation you will build day by day as you teach your child to make decisions about his or her own behavior.

Obviously, every parent wants well-behaved kids. But ideally we want our kids to choose correct behavior, to exercise self-control. That's why parents should be wary of discipline methods like those of Gary and Anne Marie Ezzo's *Growing Kids God's Way*, which rely too heavily on parental authority. Instead, look for ones that encourage the development of the child's ability to govern himself or herself.

A well-behaved child can be well-behaved for all the wrong reasons. He or she may be afraid of punishment or withdrawal of affection. This often results in a tendency to act up in awkward moments—like grocery store tantrums. And in the long run, children raised to be outer-controlled rather than self-controlled may be more vulnerable later to peer pressure and rebellion.

As Maria Montessori taught, "The first idea that the child must acquire in order to be actively disciplined is that of the difference between good and evil." And like every other potential, the potential for self-control is best released during the toddler years, when the child is eager to do things for himself or herself. The child's natural inclination is to master his or her environment. We need to help our children master themselves.

In my classroom experience and at home, I've found a simple and positive approach to self-control. A young child has little to be steward over except his or her own body. I tell my children that they are "boss" over their bodies, and then I offer them opportunities to gain greater control through "Let's See" exercises:

"Let's see if we can close the door without a sound."

"Let's see if we can walk without ringing this bell."

"Let's see how long we can sit still."

"Let's see if we can hear this pin drop."

Another effective way to help your child develop self-control is to let him or her know in advance the kind of behavior you expect—at a party, in the grocery store, in the library, or at church. When a child knows what's expected, all it takes is a glance when he or she is out of order. You know the glance I mean—not a glance that instills fear, just one that reminds a child where he or she is and what behavior is expected.

One word of caution: Construct your expectations realistically. Remember that your child is an individual and is changing all the time. Set your expectations just high enough to call forth the child's best but never too high for the child to reach. Otherwise you end up with a discouraged child.

Since children respond well to word pictures, I've used this image from the Bible to teach my own: "Like a city whose walls are broken down is a man who lacks self-control" (Prov. 25:28).

In ancient times, cities built walls to protect themselves. Any breach made them vulnerable to invasion and defeat.

The ability to control oneself is a powerful protection against self-inflicted disaster. Consider the Abu Graib soldiers whose lack of self-control made them vulnerable, resulting in great shame for themselves, their families, and their country.

In the end, training that encourages self-government rather than dependence on the presence or absence of outer control produces the kind of child people want to be around. A child with all the "selfs" our culture tries hard to foster too late and too superficially: self-awareness, self-reliance, self-confidence, and self-esteem.

When children know they can make the right decisions and are in control of their actions, all of these will follow naturally.

Then we've raised children with the right stuff.

HERE'S HELP!

Remember the power of stories?

For the child who's gone beyond emotional rumbles and spun into out-of-control, for anyone who ever had a tantrum and didn't know how to stop, there's *Where the Wild Things Are.*

Though some Christians shun this book, following the lead of one critic who claimed that it celebrates "unfettered rebellion," they're missing a really special and reassuring message for their children. Here's the real scoop:

Max misbehaves at dinner and is sent to his room. (Max has parents who care enough to punish him when necessary.)

Max sails away to an island full of Wild Things. (Max cranks up his tantrum—a "wild rumpus" with the Wild Things.)

Max, "King of All the Wild Things," finally commands them to stop. (He realizes he's in control and takes control of his emotions.)

Though the Wild Things beg him to stay, Max sails home again. (He makes the right decision.)

In his room, he finds his dinner—still warm—waiting. (He regains stability, and his parents haven't stopped loving him.)

Who hasn't been where the wild things are? Who hasn't once given into an emotional outburst and finally had to take charge? *Enough's enough!* That's what I hear Max saying, and I see his story teaching children to say that as well—all without a word of preaching or a wag of a finger.

FUN STUFF

Teaching self-control can be a lot of fun! Here's how to make it happen.

Get out in the yard with your kids for a game of "Simon Says" or "Mother, May I?" (I hope you remember—if not, go to www.games childrenplay.net)

Both of these games require kids to listen carefully and control their impulses—components of self-control. They're a great way to have fun and teach a lesson at the same time!

STEPS TO HEALTHY COMMUNICATION

THIRTEEN

"I just don't know how to deal with Paige these days," a young mother once confided in me. "Seems like she's always pouting about something. I hate to admit it, but sometimes I give in just to get things back on an even keel. Or I try to coax her out of it, and she ends up getting way too much attention. Either way, I end up feeling so manipulated!"

Allison was surprised when I told her she was already on her way to a solution. But any mom coming to grips with a problem can take heart: the first step to eliminating an unwelcome pattern is noticing it's there.

So what to do about manipulation? The first thing a frustrated parent may need is a fresh perspective. Dealing with a sulky, pouting child can bring out a host of negative parental feelings, creating enough emotional static to distort the real message.

Remember—a child doesn't intentionally set out to manipulate but resorts to pouting and other manipulative techniques when other means have failed. However, once the child discovers that these techniques work by enabling the child to get his or her way or affording otherwise unavailable attention, they may become the tools employed first in pursuit of any goal.

As William Sears observes in *Christian Parenting and Child Care,*

> At this stage of development, a child sees her interaction with her parents mainly as communication, not manipulation. Parents, avoid the tendency to overreact to your child's efforts to get what she wants. . . . When you direct her efforts to manipulate (rather than trying to squelch them), she is encouraged to communicate her needs, and she feels right in communicating them.

In short, children who manipulate are not seeking to wrest control from their parents; they are simply stuck in an immature form of communicating what they want.

Our job is then to help our children grow capable of more healthy communication. In fact, for the rest of our lives it will be up to us to see to the health of all our family communication. It starts when we tell our whining toddlers, "Use words," and continues as the children grow and try out new techniques to get what they want. What we want to do is help our children learn to understand their own feelings and put them into words in a nonoffensive way.

The following is a four-step plan you can use whenever needed to help your child develop a more mature communication pattern.

1. Step away from your feelings. When you feel frustrated by your child's sulky behavior, take a step away from the situation. Sometimes we're a little too quick to sense a power struggle where one is never intended. It's hard to have a tug-of-war when only one side is pulling a rope.

2. Step into your child's shoes. What is your child really after? Is it all about power, or is there some outcome he or she really wants? Remember—children have a limited repertoire of negotiating skills. Sometimes, pouting is the only option they can think of. Do you give your children every opportunity to express themselves constructively? Let your children know that you take their wishes into consideration and that your decision isn't just an assertion of your power.

3. Step onto your child's side of the fence. So often when our children display negative emotions, we react by stepping onto the other side of an invisible fence, and the picture becomes parent versus child. Try thinking of the struggle in terms of parent and child versus the conflict. How can the two of you resolve the current problem and move on?

4. Step through the process: Teach your children how to express themselves by offering other options, including prayer. "Honey, I know you're upset because you want to go with me today. But sticking your lip out and pouting won't change things. Use your words to tell me how you feel. You might say, 'I'm so unhappy! I wish I could go with you, Mom!' Then I would say, 'I wish you could come too, but not today.' See—when we're away from each other, I miss you too. Let's pray that God will comfort us when we have to be apart. Dear Father in heaven . . ."

All of us want our feelings to be respected. Children are no different. By teaching your children to express their feelings in constructive ways, you're giving them the tools that will be needed to handle adult conflict in a healthy manner—no pouting or manipulation with one's future spouse or children!

 FUN STUFF

Practice making faces in a mirror with your child—sad, happy, mad, scared, worried, and so on. Name the emotions as you do them. Play guessing games: "Now how am I feeling?" You guess your child's emotions; he or she can guess yours.

Now do some whining. Exaggerate. Pretend your child is Mommy and you're the child. Then say the same thing in a nice voice. Ask which one your child likes. Give the child a turn. Now which does your child like?

Pretty basic, but an important lesson is going on here about our ability to change our reactions, our tones of voice. Our children don't have much to be master of, but the following is an area in which they can take charge and decide how to act and react.

Finish up with making a poster of faces with different feelings. Or check out a poster of 30 ultra-expressive faces with labels like "curi-ous," "bored," "shocked," called "How Are You Feeling Today?" by Jim Borgman, available at www.art.com. Great fun!

 HERE'S HELP!

Are manners too old-fashioned to matter? Hardly. Far from being a lifeless set of rules, manners are keys to opening any social door. Children feel much more confident when they know what they're supposed to say and how they're supposed to act. For this reason, I highly recommend a book of manners, a little role-playing, and a lot of opportunity to practice new skills. The following are some recom-mended books.

A Little Book of Manners for Girls, by Emilie Barnes (Harvest

House, 1998), and *A Little Book of Manners for Boys*, by Bob Barnes (Harvest House, 2000). These books are written for kids 4-8 and are a good introduction to manners. But keep in mind that developing good manners in your children will take more than a book. It will take constant reinforcement.

Soup Should Be Seen, Not Heard: The Kids' Etiquette Book, by Beth Brainard and Sheila Behr (Dell, 1998). A jaunty guide to manners, including why they're important, introductions, phone etiquette, table manners, thank-you notes, dressing, grooming, personal habits, party manners, going places, and how to say "I'm sorry." Spiral-bound and very kid-friendly format.

Goops and How to Be Them: A Manual of Manners for Polite Infants Inculcating Many Juvenile Virtues Both By Precept and Example, with 90 Drawings, by Gelett Burgess (Dover Publications, republished 1968).This old-fashioned compendium of poems on manners is just plain hilarious and a fun way to review manners.

GET A GRIP ON SIBLING RIVALRY

FOURTEEN

Let's face it—the only people who can avoid sibling rivalry are parents of only children! Then again, they can't completely avoid sibling rivalry unless they themselves are only children too.

If you're in that small percentage, skip this chapter. But if sibling rivalry has ever plagued your home or continues to mess up your relationships with your own siblings, here's help. In preparation for an interview I granted for a magazine last year, I was asked several questions about this. I've left the following in question-and-answer format to keep its liveliness.

Q: How would you define the term "sibling rivalry"?

Sibling rivalry is like any rivalry we grownups experience outside our homes—so each of us is familiar with the feelings of irritation we experience sometimes in dealing with others. It's just that children wear their hearts on their sleeves and so have not developed the tools to deal with the feelings or to choose appropriate ways to express them. That's where parents come in.

Q: What causes sibling rivalry?

Fear and insecurity. And it's not just a matter of vying for parents' love, but not being fully secure in the love of our Heavenly Father. That's why all the secular parenting advice in the world won't work to eliminate sibling rivalry. If it's aimed only at making the child secure in the parents' love, there will still be that missing piece. Our security really comes from God.

Q: What are the potential benefits of healthful competition?

Healthy competition can bring out the best in everyone—kids and grownups alike. I think we must have been born with this potential, though some definitely have more of it than others. Firstborns, perhaps? I'm a firstborn, and I know nothing gets my writing juices flowing like a contest with a deadline.

Q: How do you recognize when a conflict is coming and possibly head it off before it escalates into a fight?

Believe it or not, sibling rivalry can extend into the adult years. Just last night my oldest daughters, 29 and 35—one of whom has not yet resolved her relationship with her sister—were headed for a flare-up. I stepped in and asked to discontinue the discussion. That's normally not our family style, as we do like to hash things out to completion. But our experience with these two has shown that when this pattern starts, it can quickly become unreasonable and unstoppable. I simply said, "We're not going to talk about this now."

So when you see those danger signals—and you have

the Holy Spirit to guide you, too—sometimes it just doesn't work to talk it through at the time. You need to pray first, keeping in mind Eccles. 3:7:

> *A time to tear and a time to mend,*
> *a time to be silent and a time to speak.*

Q: How does a parent know when to intervene and when to let the conflict play itself out and let the children work it out themselves?

When things get hurtful, I would intervene. Parents can teach kids that even if their feelings are strong, they should never call names or engage in vicious verbal attacks—and certainly never physical. We have very strict boundaries on hurtful behavior.

We also did not have TV for the first 15 years of our marriage—only a screen and VCR. This was specifically to avoid TV sitcoms that I felt modeled behavior I never wanted to see in my kids—sarcasm, put-downs, and humor at the expense of others. We did get TV when satellite dishes came out to pull in educational shows and football games. In recent years, we've also watched *American Idol* and *The Apprentice* and used them as springboards for discussing competition, character, and handling correction and rejection.

But I still don't let my kids watch sitcoms. And we just disconnected the television set again last month, because it seemed we were all too busy to watch it.

Anyway, I think the no- or limited-TV policy has been a major influence in shaping my kids, who are regarded as unusually kind and polite to each other as well as others.

Q: How do you resolve the situation without anyone claiming victory and without a parent taking sides? In other words, how do you find a win-win solution for all involved?

Think of something to do in common—go for a walk, go to the park, bake some cookies, make something for Daddy. Read stories about Jesus. Then talk.

However, I believe that if someone is clearly wrong, he or she needs to be confronted with it. That is to say, there isn't always a win-win situation, and if there isn't, we don't need to pretend there is.

Q: Why do you feel it's important for parents to take an active role in the relationships between their children?

Because we are their teachers. We are there to give words to their feelings and to teach them to tame them. The relationships siblings form with each other to a large extent characterize their future grown-up relationships. Unresolved issues will haunt them into adulthood. It's best to equip and empower them to understand themselves and their feelings and to deal with them in an appropriate manner.

Q: When is enough enough? At what point does sibling rivalry become unhealthful?

When a child cannot let things go, when he or she harbors resentment and cannot forgive, when he or she expects the worst from the other and is on the lookout for the other to do something wrong, when carried into adulthood and relationships with others.

Q: How do you manage to parent 12 children with unique personalities and giftings?

[See chapter 9, "It's OK to Win or Lose."] I didn't plan for all my kids to be involved in the same activity. I tried to give them all lots of opportunities to reveal how God had specifically gifted them. As an extrovert, I'm energized by others, and so I love being busy with helping each one grow.

Two of my daughters each have five children of their own. Both daughters home-school, but they're very different. I don't see one's way of doing things as superior to the other's.

One son is a contractor, one is an actor, one is studying opera, one is a National Merit Scholarship finalist planning to go into the Air Force Academy. My 16-year-old daughter is a brilliant, conscientious student. Her 13-year-old sister is a flibbertigibbet with a voice as big as Ethel Merman's and is less fond of academics than singing her heart out each day.

Then there are my four sons with Down syndrome. Three of them are adopted, so they've added more dimension with three new gene pools. One is charismatic, social, and more interested in acting and singing than learning. One is very developmentally delayed but fun-loving and happy-go-lucky. One is very interested in academics but not so great on social skills. The youngest is the life of the party and very bright in every way.

Each is so different and unique. It's a privilege and a blessing to spend this season of my life unwrapping each one like a gift from God and seeing what He's stored inside, then doing my best to help each one reach his or her potential.

HERE'S HELP

Sibling rivalry usually goes in cycles—flaring up and then settling down. When you find tension building, schedule a family meeting: "Your dad and I think we need to all sit down and talk about why you two (or three or four) are having such a tough time getting along." Ask them to come prepared to talk about what's bugging them. Start with prayer. Parents will be playing a mediator role in this. Keep in mind that some children express their hurt as anger, and their hurt feelings are just as valid as the child who cries. Listen carefully. There may be something you're doing that's causing the problem or making it worse. If so, be quick to apologize. Finish with specific commitments to change—and prayer.

FUN STUFF

Fabulously Fun Family Nights

Tired of putting a bandage on the problem of sibling rivalry? Try a proactive approach. Set aside one night a week—or one night a month if that's all you have—for family night. Turn off the television set, don't answer the phone, and just spend some good-quality time having fun. These five ideas, which just so happen to involve building each other up, will get you off to a good start:

1. Silhouettes. On a large roll of butcher paper, trace each family member's silhouette. Cut and decorate with crayons, markers, yarn, ribbon, and so on. Discuss what you like about each other's appearance. Be specific—"I love the way Emily's hair curls right under her chin."

2. Charades. Children love charades. A large family can divide into teams, but even a family of three can adapt: each person writes down the title of a song, movie, or book on a slip of paper and passes it to the second family member, who acts it out for the third. After all, it's not the competition but the zaniness that makes charades fun.

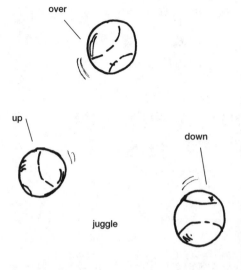

3. Juggle Mania. Find a book on juggling at the library or bookstore. Use tennis balls, oranges—whatever strikes your fancy. Help each other learn to juggle. Talk about how our lives can feel like a juggling act. What happens when something drops?

4. Make a Motto. Ask everyone in advance to be thinking of a family motto, such as "One for all and all for one." On family night discuss the possibilities, adopt one, and illustrate it on paper. A future family night could involve making a banner of your motto.

5. Acrostics: Gather all your art supplies: markers, glitter glue, stickers. Print names on slips of paper, fold, mix up, and draw. Each family member makes an acrostic for the name drawn, decorating it as beautifully as possible:

Spunky
Athletic
My brother
Up Early
Earnest
Loving

Present with a flourish. Applaud for each.

WHAT THEY REALLY NEED IS JESUS

FIFTEEN

Did you know some people believe that children are born basically good and that it is society that makes them turn bad? I used to. But then I had kids. Then I had to think through how if my sweet little daughter was born so pure of heart and I was such a loving mother doing my best to maintain her sweet little soul, how could she be such a monster sometimes?

Well, not really a monster—just a hungry, fussy, and sometimes angry bundle of needs. And then graduating to more sophisticated kinds of wrongdoing, how in the world when she was playing happily at the park could she suddenly decide she wanted to go up the slide now—"Me first!"—and push someone onto the ground to get her way?

In the back of my mind were stories I had read in high school, like William Golding's *Lord of the Flies*, in which shipwrecked boys start out organizing themselves under the leadership of a good boy but eventually fall under the sway of the bad one. If you've read it yourself, you'll know what

I mean when I say I don't even want to think about the book for more than a few seconds. But I mention it because society is not the bad guy, as many idealists think. *Oh, if he had had a better childhood, he wouldn't have murdered [robbed, assaulted, and so on].* Society is really what helps us fit into some kind of structure and stay civilized.

That was part of Golding's premise: that left to our own devices, we would degenerate to savages. I don't know if it would be as bad as all that. I mean, what if it were a group of shipwrecked nurses or nuns? But the fact is—and what I finally had to come to grips with—our human nature is flawed.

The reason for all this was a mystery to me before I became a Christian. As a New Age seeker wanting to believe in a harmonious universe, I was always at a loss to explain evil in the world. I was also at a loss to explain why my teenage daughter and I were always at odds and why my husband and I could argue over such silly and petty things as how to pack the car before a vacation.

In fact, it was at a marriage conference—my last-ditch effort to save our marriage—that I first heard what I later learned is called the Good News. And it *was* good news to me! It started with *God loves you and has a wonderful plan for your life.*

Hey—that was *very* good news! I had kind of figured out there was a God, but I thought it was this impersonal force somewhere out there. And since I was a New Ager, believing the universe was something I could work like a candy machine to get what I wanted through affirmation and visualization, it was actually exciting to hear about this God who cared about me personally and had a vision for my life.

But the good news was quickly followed by bad news: *We are separated from God by sin.*

Then more good news: *Jesus came to bridge that gap so we could know God personally.*

It was up to me: *We each have to decide whether or not to receive Jesus as Savior in order to experience God's love and His plan for our life.*

Wow! This was so simple, unlike all the esoteric spiritual practices I had been into—meditation, yoga, breathing exercises—to achieve "nirvana." Plus, I had thought of Jesus as only a spiritual teacher. Now that I knew He was the Son of God, of course I would receive Him! And that's what I prayed for instantly:

God, I'm sorry for the sin in my life, which has kept me separated from you. Thank you for sending your Son, Jesus, to give His life so that I might find new life in you. Jesus, I accept you as my Lord and Savior and give my life to your care.

I'm sharing my own story here—what Christians call "testimony"—for a reason. Though I was 38 when I became a Christian—with a degree in philosophy and many years of sophisticated spiritual seeking—when it came down to it, the moment of truth required a leap of faith that was almost childlike in its simplicity. That is, accepting Jesus as the Way, the Truth, and the Light required me to lay aside my heavy burden of adulthood and return to a place more pure and innocent.

But isn't that the way God said it would be? "Unless you change and become like little children, you will never enter the kingdom of heaven" (Matt. 18:3).

Of course, it's not as if I knew this and purposefully tried to do it this way. No, the miracle is that for an instant I stopped thinking of things like a grown-up and like a trusting child put my hand in the hand of my Heavenly Father. And while I know some people come to Christianity through the intellect—like C. S. Lewis—I'm grateful for the way God brought me.

And I share it with you like this to show that age and maturity and Bible knowledge are not prerequisites for committing your life to Christ. Mommies need to know that no one is too young to commit his or her life to Christ, and so it may well be that you will be the one to help your child do it. Why leave it to the Sunday School teachers? If you're privileged to be there at the right time with the right words, this will be another special bond you share with your child.

You can lay a foundation by teaching your child about Jesus. Include kid-level books on Bible stories in your reading repertoire. Talk to your child about God and about Jesus. Throughout the day remember to express gratitude for all the blessings God has provided for your family. This will get your child used to looking beyond his or her parents and thinking of God as the Provider.

Pray with your child. When Grandma is sick, pray for

her health. When she's well, offer a prayer of thanks. Pray for everything from finding a lost cat to being brave for a shot to getting along with a grumpy teacher.

Teach your children to pray when they are struggling. For feelings of sibling rivalry, for instance, you might say, "Let's pray and ask God to help you come and talk to Mommy when you feel like you want to hurt your sister." In this way you'll be painting a picture of how much we can depend on God to meet our needs. The time will come when the right question will elicit the response you want to hear—that first step on your child's spiritual journey.

If your family is in the habit of doing daily devotions together—which I heartily recommend, even if it's just 10 or 15 minutes before Dad goes off to work and kids go off to school—that seems like an obviously likely time when something might happen. But God isn't always on our obvious and likely timetables.

There are times when you may see your child in tremendous need of Jesus, broken and desperate and seeking some sort of reconciliation.

I've told you about my son Jonny, who has Down syndrome. His sister Maddy, who was born exactly 54 weeks after him, recently discovered the term "Irish twins" and now proudly uses it to describe them.

Because Jonny's development was a little slower, they grew up like twins—extremely close, mastering skills at the same time in the early years and going through the same issues you would expect from any siblings. Of course, in the early years there was one big difference, and that was Jonny's complete lack of guile and any behavior that might hurt someone. I remember one summer day catching Maddy, then four or five, picking on Jonny. She was sentenced to time-out on the bench we used for such occasions. She was so ashamed and mortified—you know how sometimes we're more convicted when we're caught doing something wrong.

Through her tears, I remember her expressing how helpless she felt about her bad behavior. "I love Jonny," she said. "I don't know why I'm mean to him sometimes."

I knelt down next to the bench and told her what it means to have sin in your life. She says she remembers my telling her that Satan wanted her to be mean to Jonny and that she should tell Satan to go away. I told her that the reason she could not change her behavior was because she was trying to do it herself, that if she really wanted to change, she needed to ask Jesus into her heart.

Did she want to ask Jesus into her heart and be able to trust God to help her live a better life?

"Yes," she cried. And so I just prayed a simple prayer with her to do that.

Maddy remembers that moment today.

While skeptics might say that the child follows the will of the parents and makes this commitment whether he or she means it or not, I disagree. One of our children repeatedly said no when asked whether he wanted to commit his life to Christ. Only after several years did he finally break one night over something and take that step. And though he was only six, he cried a river of tears of joy and relief when he did so. We were so overjoyed that we woke all the siblings to share the wonderful news.

Will having Jesus in their hearts make a difference? Rest assured it will! You will definitely see better behavior and a genuine difference in your home. And now when there's trouble or bad behavior, things aren't so hopeless, because you're dealing with someone governed by the Holy Spirit, whose heart is teachable.

When a home is filled with believers—not just Mom and Dad, but everyone—there's more peace and joy. I promise.

HERE'S HELP!

The following books will plant seeds as you in your daily living nurture the soil of your child's heart. At the right time and place, something wonderful will begin to grow.

Read-Aloud Bible Stories, Volumes 1-4, and *Parables Jesus Told*, by Ella K. Lindvall (Moody Press, 1982-2000). These large volumes with bold, full-page illustrations on one side and simple text on the other have a lot of kid appeal. One unusual feature is that Jesus' face is never seen, thus avoiding some of the stereotypes and allowing room for children's imaginations. Bible stories are retold with rhythm, repetition, and loads of enthusiasm.

Giant Steps for Little People, by Kenneth N. Taylor (Tyndale House, 1985). The Sermon on the Mount and the Ten Commandments are broken into bite-sized morsels a very young child can grasp and grow on. Each page offers a spiritual truth, a practical application (with lots of opportunities for parent-child conversation), a prayer, and a memory verse.

Little People in Tough Spots: Bible Answers for Young Children, by V. Gilbert Beers (Thomas Nelson, 1992). This gem of a book shows children in an easy-to-understand way that the answers to life's problems are in the Bible. Pick a problem—I'm scared, I have too much to do, Do I have to share?—and you'll find a vignette of a child here and now who faces the problem, then draws inspiration from a particular person in the Bible.

Read-n-Grow Picture Bible, by Jim Padgett (Tommy Nelson, 2003). A total of 1,872 illustrations (six per page, with a sentence or two under each) will take your child through the Bible from start to finish. My kids have loved this motivational format, which has really reinforced the historical continuity of the Bible.

 ## MOVIE DATE

Many movies have been made about Jesus, but one I really like is the one produced and distributed by The JESUS Film Project, a division of Campus Crusade for Christ, in which virtually every word spoken by Jesus is directly from the Gospel of Luke. Watch it together as a family, and talk about it together. This may be a catalyst for your child to make a decision for Christ. A children's version is also available. Find more information at <www.jesusfilm.org>.

Less is more——really.

NO TIME TO BE CHOOSY

SIXTEEN

Long ago when I was a latchkey kid, I would come home from school and find a few dollars and a grocery list from Mama. I would walk down the street to the store, load a basket, cross my fingers that I would have enough money not to have to put anything back, and then carry my bounty home in a double brown bag.

Forty-some years later I shop in a suburban megamarket a few acres wide, strolling through aisles brimming with food fit for a queen: a dozen apple varieties, a hundred imported cheeses, an astonishing array of exotic breads and gourmet ice creams.

These days, grocery shopping is more an art form than a survival tactic. But sometimes I wonder if we've really gained much at all.

It hit me one morning when I was shopping. In a mustard aisle meltdown, I nearly collapsed beneath the weight of all my choices. A multitude of specialty items—my cart in standby mode, my hand reaching, then hesitating, the labels becoming a blur. So many mustards, so little time!

I experienced similar panic that afternoon at the post office trying to buy 100 37-cent stamps (back before they went to 39 cents). The clerk whipped out a vast selection that included Andy Warhol, birthday candles, Mary Cassatt mini-artworks, 9/11 scenes, and creepy-crawly reptiles. Which would be the perfect expression of me?

That evening found me in the throes of comparing cell phone rate plans when my son interrupted with a veritable catalogue of design-your-own class rings—12 models, 10 colors, five cuts of stones, and 50 (count 'em!) possible side engravings. The selection took us an hour.

Overcome with nostalgia, I spent the rest of the evening tracking down my own high school ring. The stone was blue, the sides engraved with my high school insignia, and 1965. That year our only choice was to order the boy's ring or the more diminutive girl's version.

I don't remember feeling shortchanged at all.

Yes, we're surrounded by choices fit for queens, but some days the crown lies heavier than others. The truth is, choosing takes time, and for a busier-each-day mommy, time grows more precious each day.

I remember with fondness that teeny corner store where I chose between white bread and brown, red apples and green, American and Swiss, dill and sweet. Only two mustards graced the shelf then: the regular and its first racy cousin. Today I grab the original like a lifeline and hightail it to the checkout line, where at least they've finally stopped asking me if I want paper or plastic.

My mother used to tell me, "Beggars can't be choosy." But that's not the problem today, when picking out a time-saver or working out some problems with your Internet browser can take so much time you wonder why you thought these things would improve the quality of your life. Just picking out the right diapers or car seat or riding toy for your child can take way too long for comfort.

Don't you sometimes just wish there weren't so many choices? I mean, you would never know the difference, and think how much time you would save!

To tell you the truth, if I had my druthers now, I would take time over almost anything that diverts my attention from the things that truly matter.

That's why, when it comes to options, sometimes less is more.

 HERE'S HELP!

Half a Dozen Timesavers

- Use a Crock-Pot. In the morning, throw in boneless chicken thighs and spaghetti sauce; or a piece of meat, condensed mushroom soup, and Lipton's onion soup mix. Half an hour before dinner, boil some pasta.
- Put off going to the grocery store as long as you can. If you have a grocery store delivery service, use it. I pay a $5 delivery charge where I live, but it's worth every penny for the gas I save, not to mention the stuff I would have bought that wasn't on my list—and all the time it would have taken. If your hubby likes to do Costco or Sam's Club, send him with a list, and—again—save time and money.
- Carpool not just to school but to extracurricular activities.
- Sort through the mail once only. Throw away every catalogue and every piece of advertising. Open everything you need, and throw away the outer envelope and all extra stuff. Keep only what you need to pay your bill or reply to or file.
- Give your kids chores. Actually, teaching them to serve others is as good for them as receiving their help is good for you.

- Don't answer every phone call. Sometimes the message left is all you need. If you have to call back, tell the person if you have only five or so minutes to talk.

Inspiration

What Did I Do Today?
What did I do today?
Today I left some dishes dirty,
The bed got made around 3:30.
The diapers soaked a little longer,
The odor grew a little stronger.
The crumbs I spilled the day before
Are staring at me from the floor.
The fingerprints there on the wall
Will likely be there still next fall.
The dirty streaks on those window panes
Will still be there next time it rains.

"Shame on you," you sit and say,
"Just what did you do today?"

I nursed a baby till he slept,
I held a toddler while she wept.
I played a game of hide-and-seek,
I squeezed a toy so it would squeak.
I pulled a wagon, sang a song,
Taught a child right from wrong.
What did I do this whole day through?
Not much that shows—I guess that's true,
Unless you think that what I've done
Might be important to someone
With bright brown eyes and soft brown hair.
If that is true—I've done my share.
—Author Unknown

BACK TO BASICS—
TOY-WISE

SEVENTEEN

With all the kids I have at my house, I know how tempting toy stores—even the online variety—can be. And I know that when I first became a parent, maybe *especially* because I had grown up poor and felt that everyone had more stuff than I could ever dream of, I way overdid it in buying things for my kids.

But I've come a long way, baby. With as many kids as we have and as many birthdays—not to mention Christmas—we eventually ended up with way too much stuff. And if there's one thing that feels worse than not enough, it's too much.

Plus I had seen over and over that the cutest and most must-have stuff I loaded into my cart and brought home ended up with a limited life span. And then I would have the big dilemma about whether to let it go to Goodwill to find its way into the hands of someone who would appreciate it more than my kids. But why didn't my kids appreciate it?

I don't know the answer to that one, but over the years I've learned what works and what doesn't with kids. It doesn't take a rocket scientist to see that our babies would rather play with the Tupperware and measuring spoons and Mommy's purse than the latest bells-and-whistles super-toy on television. They would rather get into Mommy's makeup and Daddy's shaving cream than anything that actually cost their parents something at the store.

And so when mommies ask me, "What should I buy my kids?" I just say—as I have in other areas of my life—sometimes less is more.

Here's a typical question from a MommyLife reader (that's my blog—<www.mommylife.net>):

What type of toys would you recommend for an older baby or toddler? I really want stuff that will teach him motor skills, but I don't want to clutter up the house.

My reply:

Here are things time-tested in the Curtis house (12 kids over 36 years—like my own scientific laboratory. Does that mean I could be considered a rocket scientist on raising kids?)

A Fisher Price or Little Tykes dollhouse and family figures

A little farm with animals and a farmer

A doll baby

Brio trains (or a less expensive knock-off)

Duplos (the forerunner to Legos—made for pudgy little hands

Legos later on—boys love them

A toy shopping cart

A child-sized play kitchen

A set of wooden blocks

Other than these items, I would concentrate on learning materials that you are less likely to find in toy aisles and more likely to find in a teacher's supply store in your area or online. Professionals call these "manipulatives," and they are designed to encourage a child to focus, concentrate, and perfect his or her fine motor skills.

A pegboard

Lacing cards

Puzzles with knobs

A stacking tower

A sorting exercise

Introduce these one at a time, slowly and carefully showing your child how to use them (complete instructions are at <www.mommylife.net>). Always encourage your child to repeat an activity as many times as possible before he or she grows tired of it. That builds your child's concentration. Then put it away before getting out something else.

Don't allow these items to be treated carelessly or jumbled up in a toy box. Keep each set neatly on a shelf, teaching your child to take one set off, carry it to a table, use it, then put it away. If your child isn't ready to deal with that, put the items away in a closet, and get them out and put them away as needed.

Back in chapter 4, "It's Their House Too," we talked about the importance of preparing an environment that would meet your children's needs and encourage them to find things to do. Here we're just adding an extra dimension: taking a little extra time to show them how to do things until they can do them independently.

When you have a few well-chosen items, and your children know how to use them properly and can work independently and concentrate, you won't need scads of toys around. Remember—scads of toys mean lots of clutter and lots more housework. Who needs that?

Hopefully your children love books and have an organized place to keep them and a comfy place to read them. A bunch of dress-up clothes is wonderful for imaginative play. Hooks are better than a basket so the clothes can be picked out without making a mess.

Honestly, that's just about all they really need.

Except for you, of course!

HERE'S HELP!

Providing your kids with an afternoon of fun can be as simple as putting some sheets over the dining room table so they can pretend to go camping.

Here are some great Internet sites for more ideas:

Homemade Toys and Printable Games:
<www.first-school.ws/theme/hometoys.htm>

Twenty Toys You Don't Have to Buy:
<www.shmonster.com/old_site/twenty_toys.html>

Robyn's Nest:
<www.robynsnest.com/homemade.htm>

All About Coloring:
<www.coloring.ws>

Kids' Turn Central:
<www.kidsturncentral.com/crafts/craftrecipes.htm>

Blocks—arrange to make things

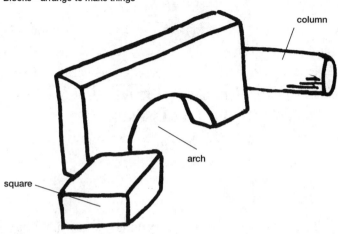

FUN STUFF

While it's fun to live off the beaten track, living on a dirt road has its downside: a constantly dirty car. Add to that the fact that I often have to pack the little kids up to drop the older kids off at their evening activities, then be available to pick them up an hour later, and you know I have some time to kill.

But aside from playing the Wiggles and Raffi CDs and singing along at the top of our lungs, the other night I found a great diversion for the little kids.

I plunked down $8 for the super deluxe wash, because that meant more back and forths and lots of color with the bubble wax. If you asked my sons, they would say it was the best $8 Mommy ever spent.

I don't know which is better, having a clean car at last or the happy memories of Jonny, Jesse, Daniel, and Justin as dazzled as if we had been on a Disney ride—and all without enduring the long lines and frazzled families!

It's your local carwash. Check it out for a cheap thrill!

BRINGIN' 'EM UP WITH THE BE'S

EIGHTEEN

Big families have more of everything—more lunchboxes, laundry, and loose teeth. We make more beds, wash more dishes, tie more shoes. We need more patience, haircuts, and Happy Meals.

What we don't need is more rules.

One thing we have less of is time. And because lots of rules take lots of time to teach and enforce, I streamlined ours to "The Three Be's."

The Three Be's is our family's straight and narrow, a path to joyful living we've charted for our kids. Now when their behavior strays, a simple, "Be . . ." is all it takes to nudge them back on track.

Be grateful.

It's hard to go wrong when your heart is giving thanks. Maybe that's why the Bible reminds us so often!

- Teach your kids that God is their true Provider. Food, clothing, and home don't come from you but through you—from God.

- Play tapes of praise and thanksgiving in the car and during housework.
- Find ways to be grateful even for chores. Setting the table reminds us that we have plenty to eat. Folding laundry reminds us that we have nice clothes to wear.
- Model gratitude for your kids by noting even the small things God has done for you.

Be of service.

Children have a natural inclination to serve. Nurture it. When they're little and want to help, don't shoo them away —show them how!

- Children are little mirrors. Make sure they see you serving with a smile.
- Be a team. If it takes one person four hours to clean the house, it takes four only one. That's three hours left for fun.
- Find ways to serve your community, such as picking up litter, recycling, visiting seniors.
- Share stories of the Good Samaritan, Mary breaking her alabaster jar, Jesus washing the disciples' feet.
- Appreciate their efforts. Give them hugs and kisses.

Be the best you can be.

They'll never be perfect, but we want our kids to be the best they can be in action and character. Simply by pointing kids in a positive direction, a lot of negative can be eliminated.

- Remind them often that God loves them and has a special plan for each of them, one that even Mom and Dad are waiting to discover.

- Assure your kids that we're not made from a cookie cutter. Not everyone will be a pro ballplayer or ballerina, but each has special gifts and abilities.
- Encourage your kids to look at their weaknesses honestly by sharing some of your own.
- Forgive mistakes quickly, making it clear that God can use them to help us learn.
- Motivate your kids by noticing even the smallest efforts in the right direction.

The Three Be's are not an exhaustive study, but they're not exhausting either. Children catch on quickly.

But what I like best is that there are only three. And when I'm mentally rattling through multiple names to get one child's attention—"Benja . . . , Matth . . . , Zacha . . . , Joshua!"—by the time I catch my breath, it's a relief to say "Be . . ." and have just three to choose from!

 FUN STUFF

Five More Fabulously Fun Family Nights

1. Songfest at the Sea (or nearest body of water). Find a song-book of old Americana ("My Darling Clementine," "Sweet Betsy from Pike," "Shoo Fly") at the library. Take a light dinner (as simple as bread, cheese, and fruit) to the beach; then snuggle in blankets and sing by sunset or flashlight.

2. Winter Picnic. (For the coldest weather) Cut out a big yellow sun and hang it on the wall. Spread a checkered tablecloth on the floor. Wear shorts. Serve hot dogs or chicken, potato salad, deviled eggs. Plan your summer vacation.

3. Family Tree. Share any information you have about your ancestors with your children. Draw a family tree. As a family, write what you would want your own future descendants to know about you. What are your strongest family values?

4. Memory Lane. Fill a large tray with family objects: toothpaste tube, baby bottle, small teddy bear, scissors, pen, watch, and so on. Give everyone paper and pencil, then uncover the tray and let them look for 60 seconds. Cover the tray, and have everyone write the names of as many objects as they can remember. Why did each family member remember certain things? What will you remember most about your family?

5. Moonlight Walk. Go for a walk in the moonlight. Whisper.

A WORN-OUT WELCOME

NINETEEN

Ever had a guest you wish you hadn't invited? Maybe you were looking forward to a little fun and found a lot of wasted time instead. If so, maybe you'll tune right in to this picture of an ungracious guest.

He dominates the room, grabbing attention whenever he can.

But a little attention is never enough; he's always demanding more. He monopolizes time and conversations, making it difficult to get a word in edgewise. His voice is too loud, his manners pathetic. He swears and takes God's name in vain, has little respect for family ties, pokes fun at things that matter deeply, tells off-color jokes in front of the children.

Yet he's one of the most popular guests in town. Despite his atrocious manners, his calendar is full—all day, all night, weekdays, weekends, rain or shine, in sickness or in health.

And he doesn't discriminate. You'll find him in the poorest homes and the richest, among the happy and the miserable—all ages, races, and colors.

Maybe you've spent some time with this ill-mannered guest yourself. Maybe sometimes you wish you hadn't.

Somehow he seems to mix up your priorities. You find he's rubbed off on you, putting words into your mouth that weren't there before. You hear yourself being sarcastic or mean to family. You find yourself distracted from the ideals you've set for yourself.

So why do you keep turning on the tube?

Even moms who are picky about who their children play with often have a blind spot where television is concerned. But moms can't afford any blind spots.

Moms, if you want the best for your kids, you must think ahead. By using TV as a pacifier/entertainer for your kids, you may be gaining a few minutes of relief, but you'll be selling your kids and your family short.

First of all, your children will never learn to entertain themselves but will always be dependent on an outside source.

Second, you'll miss important moments of bonding. The secret of *quality* time is that you're more likely to have it if you have lots of *quantity* time.

Third, you'll be leaving your children wide open to forces working to create a consumer mentality as early as possible. By the time they're teens, they'll be like sheep following as materialism beckons.

It's much better to put a stool in the kitchen and let your child climb up to watch you at work. Let your child put away the dishes and wipe the counters, even if he or she can't do it very well. Let your child help you move the clothes from the washer and dryer. Make your child feel like an important and necessary member of the family. This will build more self-esteem than a lifetime of Barney.

I really encourage moms who've been using TV to think more long-term. You want kids who are cheerful, unselfish, helpful, and who can find things to do independently. Every minute watching TV sets them back from those goals.

 ## MOMMY POWER

American children and adolescents spend 22 to 28 hours per week viewing television, more than any other activity except sleeping.
By the age of 70 they will have spent 7 to 10 years
of their lives watching TV.
—The Kaiser Family Foundation

Protestant clergy named divorce, negative influences from the media, and materialism as the three greatest threats
to families in their communities.
—From an Ellison Research study of 695 Protestant church ministers nationwide, October 2004

It might make you feel differently about how much TV you want your kids to watch if you consider that the products TV is interested in selling are its viewers, not the things you see in the commercials. Or put another way, the programs on TV are a lure to hook viewers so that advertisers can buy time to sell them their products. I don't know about you, but having my children viewed as consumers rather than people really creeps me out. I keep TV to a minimum.

 ## MAKING CHANGES

You may not be willing to give up TV entirely, but here are a few suggestions.

No TV during meals. Meals are a time for the family to interact and children to learn to use good manners and make conversation. Sample discussion starters:

"If you could invite to dinner any person from any time in history, who would it be, and what would you talk about?"

"If you could go anywhere in the world, where would it be, and what would you do there?"

"If you found a million dollars in a suitcase, what would you do? If the owners were never found and it was given to you, what would you do with it?"

"What has been the best day of your life? What would be your perfect day?"

Did you know that students with higher SAT scores have one thing in common across all economic and social divides? They sit down for family dinner—and I'm guessing without the tube.

No TV sets in bedrooms. Create more family time and togetherness by reserving bedrooms for sleeping and down time—not computers or TV.

Get out of the automatic tendency to turn on the tube. Play some board games as a family. Try jigsaw puzzles or crossword puzzles. Give your kids a bunch of old magazines to cut out pictures and make a collage. Take a walk at night. Lie out on the lawn on a warm night and look at the stars. As Robert Louis Stevenson wrote,

> *The world is so full of a number of things*
> *I'm sure we should all be as happy as kings.*

Don't let TV get in the way of finding out all those wonderful things God has created and all the wonderful ways we can build our family relationships!

SOME THINGS ARE
BETTER LEFT UNDONE

TWENTY

A question from a MommyLife reader:

I have three very young children: A three-year-old (who is delayed), a two-year-old, and a four-month-old. I'm having difficulty figuring out how our day should be scheduled so as to meet all their needs, keep them entertained, and be able to get my way-too-numerous chores done.

My reply:

Sometimes these simple questions have a way of bringing me to my knees. Because to tell you the truth, there are so many mommies who can identify—and I was once there myself—it seems like a miracle that we ever made it through. Yet we do.

Anne Lamott wrote, "It's not just that I believe in miracles—I rely on them." We would probably do well to start every day reminding ourselves that we're depending on God for all the miracles we need to remain patient and calm and make the right choices—and the miracle of being able to forgive ourselves when we fall short.

I think the biggest struggle for me was letting go of the goal of keeping my house in perfect order. I really didn't learn until my fifth child that it wasn't as important as I had thought. When your children are young and you're solely responsible for the house, some things may have to go for a while. As they get older, your children become part of the team that takes care of the house, and then things are much easier. But in the early years, you can make yourself crazy trying to do the impossible. And then motherhood is no fun.

If I could do one thing over, I would play more with my kids. Even though your kids aren't much help at this age, you can give them little "chores" to do—even just a cloth to "clean off the cabinets" while you clean the kitchen. Tell them you can all do your work first, then play. Then when you're finished with the kitchen, instead of feeling compelled to do the next room, really take some time and play with them.

Whenever possible, take them outside to play. If you don't have a yard, go to a park. That has the dual advantage of getting them out of the house to prevent further messes and helping them get the exercise and fresh air that will stabilize them physically so they can have some quiet time at home. When you come home, make it a habit to give them a snack and then have that quiet time—maybe look at board books or listening to music or watch a worthwhile video.

Read lots of books to them.

When you're cooking, rather than turning them over to

the TV, get them up on stools to watch what you're doing. Maybe they can scrub carrots or do another activity that will give them the feeling of making a contribution. Sing with them as you work. Play classical music to calm everyone's nerves.

Dance with them. Bounce balls. Blow bubbles.

The more you play with them, the more they learn how to play. But do insist on times when they're responsible for their own entertainment, promising some time together after.

At the same time, try to help your kids become independent as quickly as possible. That is, not independent of you and your love for them or their need to obey, but independent in terms of doing whatever they can for themselves.

Here's my general rule of thumb for how anything from sweeping the floor to buttoning a shirt gets done in our house:

Four Questions

Can the child do it alone? Is your child able to dress himself or herself? To clean his or her room? To clean up his or her own place after breakfast? Then that's what should happen. This first question is related to independence, and though it does not mean that you should be rigid (it's OK and part of role modeling to help others), the rule of thumb is this: If the child can do it alone, let the child do it.

Can someone younger do it? As I mentioned before, I've always kept my dishes in the lower cabinets so my children could be involved in taking them out of the dishwasher and putting them away as well as setting the table. But my confidence in delegating chores was ratcheted up a few notches when Jonny and Maddy, at two and three years old, barely toddlers and anxious to copy their older brothers and sisters, began taking on this chore themselves. This is one of the perks of a big family: once you get past the everyone-needs-Mommy stage, you have lots and lots of help.

There are chores even the smallest can do. Don't ask your eight-year-old to bring a diaper for the baby if your three-year-old is around. The younger child will relish the opportunity to serve, and the older child is capable of more advanced assignments. For big cleanups and small, work is distributed according to one principle: Delegate any task to the youngest capable of doing it.

Can it be done differently? You may have grown up with a mother who was so perfect that she ironed your jeans. Or maybe she *didn't* iron jeans, but your friend's mother did, and you wondered why your mother didn't. Anywhere along the line, you may have picked up some ideas of perfection that just aren't adding much to your life.

Ever hear the story about the young wife who argued with her husband each Thanksgiving because she cut the turkey in half to roast it? When he insisted that it wasn't necessary, she asked her mother why she had grown up with Thanksgiving turkeys cut in half. Mom, who couldn't remember seeing a whole turkey in her own childhood, had to go to Grandma to find out why. Grandma was amazed at the legacy she had passed on. And so were her daughter and granddaughter when she told them that she had always cut the turkey in half because her oven was too small, and each year's turkey was too big to cook the normal way.

What doesn't fit in your oven? Are you doing things in ways that are unnecessary or too exacting for your family?

The following is a personal example based on the perpetual laundry situation at our house.

Early in my motherhood I began to notice that children have a tough time keeping clothes neatly folded in their drawers. For a while I was frustrated at the time I had wasted folding. Then it occurred to me that folding could be a much more informal affair than I had ever imagined.

This will explain my current, casual routine: As I empty the dryer, I hang whatever goes on hangers and quickly (nothing fancy) fold big items like jeans, T-shirts, and pajamas in stacks, one per child. The children periodically come and get their stacks to put away in their rooms. In the meantime, the small items of clean laundry such as socks, underwear, and napkins accumulate in the laundry baskets until they are full. Just before it does, I call all the children, turn on some music, and dump the clothes onto the carpeted floor of my bedroom. They fold together until it's all done, and then everyone puts everything away.

I use this chore as an example and share it in such detail to reveal how chores don't have to be done the way your mother did them or the way your neighbor does them. They can instead be tailored to your family, keeping your priorities in mind. My goal with the laundry was to get a very large and very necessary job done without unnecessary stress while promoting the joy of serving together as a family.

My choice involved modifying my standards about how folded clothes should look. But it was a choice I made willingly. At the time I made this decision, nine of my children were under 13, most of them not capable of folding to perfection. But as I said, clothes in children's drawers never seem to stay folded for long. And I've noticed wrinkled T-shirts have a way of smoothing out when my boys put them on anyway.

Keep in mind that modifying your standards is not always a sign of laziness but sometimes of intelligent decision-making. When we lower our standards because circumstances defeat us or we feel weak, we don't feel good about the result. But when we evaluate the demands on our time, our children's capabilities, and our family's priorities, a decision to temporarily modify our standards in some area may actually be the most responsible path, which leads me to the last question concerning housework.

Does it need to be done at all? When my fifth child came along, I began streamlining what I thought was necessary. The process went something like this: "Do the dishes need to be hand-dried and put away immediately, or can they air-dry overnight?" The chores that were dropped were evidently of such small consequence that I can't even remember what they were.

A writer writes best from experience, and this was mine: I wanted my house to look nice. I wanted a lot of children. Though not mutually exclusive desires, pursuing both created some tension. Resolving that tension involved some compromise. Reaching that compromise took some time.

But I didn't have anyone to tell me better. You do! If your perfectionism about your house has been keeping you from enjoying yourself as a mother, see what you can let go. Take baby steps. Pray to God for wisdom. On the other hand, if your problem is lack of motivation or disorganization, make a big initial push to get your house in order—decluttering and making a fresh start—and then try to maintain a reasonable grasp on it without letting it completely fall apart. Keep in mind that God didn't make us from cookie cutters, so each of us has our own set of character issues we need to work on. Take it one day at a time.

When you start to get discouraged, just remember this is a very short season in your life, though while you're in it, I know it feels like forever. Soon those little ones will be real helpers you and their father can count on. Then you'll wonder how it happened so fast.

 MOMMY POWER

Ten-Minute Pickups
By the Curtis Kids

No, this isn't a health drink or aerobic exercise, but a way of life at the Curtis house.

Several times a day, whenever Mom feels that things are getting too crazy clutterwise, she calls for a "ten-minute pickup." Probably anyone could call for a pickup, but no one else seems to care as much as Mom.

This is our signal to drop what we're doing and look for things that need to be put away. Sometimes she's desperate; then she calls for a 20-minute pickup.

We work together, and soon everything is cleaned up. The little lines between Mom's eyebrows disappear. She says this is the key to her sanity.

God sure makes moms different, but it's worth whatever it takes to keep them happy.

Inspiration

Counting

Count your blessings instead of your crosses,
Count your gains instead of your losses,
Count your joys instead of your woes,
Count your friends instead of your foes.
Count your courage instead of your fears,
Count your laughs instead of your tears.
Count your full years instead of your lean,
Count your kind deeds instead of your mean.
Count your health instead of your wealth,
Count on God instead of yourself.

—Author unknown

When the going gets tough, just keep going.

BE PREPARED
FOR MIRACLES
TWENTY-ONE

Five summers ago I almost lost a son.

I was finishing up errands when I got the call on my cell phone. My five-year-old son, Jesse, was in trouble: a near-drowning. Helicopter on its way. No time for me to get there. Call back in five minutes to find out which hospital.

I hung up, not quite breathing, alone with all the questions: How had this happened? Had someone forgotten to lock the gate?

Would he live? Jesse's sweet smile, almond eyes, and silky brown skin seemed suddenly more real, more necessary than the sidewalk under my feet. The emergency medical technician had said something about brain damage. Oh, woe if Jesse—already challenged with Down syndrome —should have to work harder than he already did!

Five minutes later, Jesse was whirring above the San Francisco Bay to Children's Hospital in Oakland. Thank God he would be there before I could even get onto the freeway. With no traffic, it would take me an hour—time to reassure my kids via cell phone and to hear the whole story.

Jesse hadn't been alone. Everyone was swimming, but no one heard when he had somehow slipped off the seat in the hot tub where little kids like to hang out. He went under without a sound.

My oldest son, Josh, spotted him and pulled him out like a soggy rag doll. Jesse's skin was blue, his eyes rolled back, his chest still.

"We need to do CPR!" Matt yelled.

And the two oldest brothers went to work—opening the airway, giving two quick breaths, checking for the pulse. Then, because there was no pulse, they began chest compressions. Ben called 911. Thank God that Josh and Matt knew CPR!

And here's why those inclined to believe in God's provision see life filled with more intentional meaning than those who think in terms of simple twists of fate: In 1995 Tripp and I had to pass a CPR course in order to adopt Jesse. For some strange reason we decided to have our whole family trained. I say strange, because at the time Josh and Matt were only 12 and 11, we had no pool, and recreational water play consisted of blowing up an inflatable circle, filling it with a few inches of water, then spending hours looking for leaks. Not much chance of drowning there.

Now, five years later, Josh and Matt saved Jesse's life—this according to the emergency medical technicians who converged on our house, rounded up the kids, secured the dogs, called me, and arranged for Jesse's transport.

Still I think there's a little something else involved.

I already shared that quote from Anne Lamott, but it

seems so appropriate and I love it so much that I need to share it again here: "It's not just that I believe in miracles; I rely on them." This is really my mainstay philosophy as a mommy, as well as the words of Job in the Bible: "He performs wonders that cannot be fathomed, miracles that cannot be counted" (Job 5:9; 9:10).

In Jesse's story I see a few miracles myself. He regained consciousness after 27 hours and then developed a virulent pneumonia. The going was slow until his fourth day, Sunday, when after a particularly cranky, distressing morning, Jesse suddenly sat up, smiled, and wanted to play. A week later he was completely well.

Our CPR instructor was amazed. Though he had been training people for 15 years, this was a first for him. What's more, even in his primary job as a firefighter, he'd arrived on thousands of accident scenes and never seen someone already doing CPR.

And though he himself had initiated CPR on 26 of those scenes, none of the victims survived.

That's because it was too late. The first five minutes after someone stops breathing is critical—too short a time to wait for the professionals. Since 75 percent of the time the person who needs CPR will be someone you know, knowing how to help means more safety for your family.

It did for ours.

Jesse, whose name means "God exists," almost died—and didn't. But sometimes miracles aren't as simple as they look. Sometimes they depend on decisions we've made before.

Thank God we decided to have our family trained in CPR.

Inspiration

Miracles are a retelling in small letters of the very same story which is written across the whole world in letters too large for some of us to see.
—C. S. Lewis

There are no miracles for those that have no faith in them.
—French Proverb

*There are only two ways to live your life.
One is as though nothing is a miracle. The other
is as though everything is a miracle.*
—Albert Einstein

Where there is great love there are always miracles.
—Willa Cather

*To me every hour of the day and night
is an unspeakably perfect miracle.*
—Walter Chrysler

 FUN STUFF

Movie Date

The Miracle Worker (skip any remakes and go straight to the 1962 classic) is a must-see for every family. If you haven't seen it since you were a kid, you'll get so much out of it now watching it with your own children. And if you've never seen it, you've missed two of the greatest female movie performances ever: Patty Duke as Helen Keller and Anne Bancroft as Annie Sullivan, the young woman determined to reach beyond Helen's deafness and blindness to touch Helen's soul, which was not handicapped at all. *The Miracle Worker* speaks loud and clear of how important we ourselves sometimes can be in carrying out the miracles God intends for others.

HELPING KIDS MAKE SENSE OF DISASTERS

TWENTY-TWO

While there have always been disasters, recent years have brought us several of monumental proportions: the September 11, 2001, terrorist strikes; the 2004 day-after-Christmas tsunami; and Hurricane Katrina and its horrible aftermath in 2005. Add the fact that we now have news crews there within minutes or hours and round-the-clock live coverage even as we're trying to grapple with the enormity of the loss. Do you, like me, feel overwhelmed by the contrast as you go about your normal daily life of doing laundry, making peanut butter sandwiches, and trying to balance the checkbook as though somehow we're untouched by the devastation of our neighbors?

In the wake of these disasters, thinking of the enormity of the tragedy and personal loss others face actually hurt my heart. Would you understand if I said I wanted it to hurt my children's hearts too?

I've always had this thing about not getting too comfortable, always felt compelled to teach my kids not to take our security and material blessings for granted. For years

I've cut out *National Geographic* pictures of children all over the world—eager African children crowded in ramshackle classrooms, kids coming home from market with bunches of fish on their heads, squatting on a dirt floor to shape tortillas with Mama, herding sheep with Papa. Like the ticker running at the bottom of the news channel screen, they hang at kids'-eye-level throughout our house, subliminal reminders that our American lifestyle isn't really the norm.

As a Montessori teacher, I was taught to introduce to children at an early age the diversity of the world through striking visual images.

I was also trained to look at things through children's eyes. And so when a cataclysmic event occurs, my first thought is with them.

My advice for parents:

- Do all you can to make this a meaningful event for your children and to manage the meaning in a way that will build their character, their compassion, and their willingness to sacrifice for those in need.

- Watch the news coverage with them, putting the images into words. Don't let your little ones be blindsided by glimpses of dead bodies, weeping parents, and looting on television or in the newspaper or magazines. Without your intervention, these images can produce deep fears that children have no language to share.

- Show them on a map where you live and where the disaster struck.

- Teach them to give in a way that involves real sacrifice on their part. Put a jar in the middle of the table—a constant visual reminder—and fill it with change that would have gone to sweets or movie rentals or something currently taken for granted. Young children can comprehend the abstract only when we make it concrete. The sight of the jar, the sound of the change hitting the glass—these seem insignificant to us, but they're sensory cues that will shape memories for children of their first sacrificial giving.

- Be sure to share with them about the thousands of ordinary people on their way now to help—soldiers, Red Cross and Salvation Army relief workers, medical professionals, all kinds of people willing to drop everything and go help those in need. Remind them that our country is known for this kind of personal sacrifice and generosity. Show them pictures of the tents and mass food service and, as it begins, the reconstruction.

- Above all, read to them or tell them the stories of survivors. While it's too early for these to appear, over the coming weeks they will. Then be sure to look for stories of courage and selflessness, along with stories of those who saved lives. Look for stories that show God's mercy, and let your children know that we can find reassurance from these small glimpses into God's character.

Basically, the idea is not to ignore what's going on. Your children are sure to be affected by the bits and snippets of news swirling around them, and they often do not have the ability to put their fears into words. Think of how a child of divorce believes himself or herself to be responsible and hides that terrible fear in his or her heart. Our role as parents is to help our kids make sense of reality and then point them in a positive direction with the stories of those who help and those who survive.

Who knows what our kids will face in the future? I know I want mine prepared, unhindered by my shortcomings, and ready to help others face whatever lies ahead.

As parents, we recognize that our job is to instill a message of hope, reinforcing in our children the habit of turning in that direction when times are tough. That's why if we have a tendency to hopelessness, we must—and I rarely use the word "must"—work extra hard to become hopeful ourselves in order to pass it on to our kids.

The main thing that will help our kids should they ever experience such devastation in their own lives is a solid foundation in faith. Teach them to love Jesus and to trust God with all their hearts and minds and strength. Help them learn as many Bible verses as possible, for those will be treasures hidden in their hearts.

 HERE'S HELP!

The American Bible Society's web site, Constant Hope (<www.con stanthope.org>), offers e-cards with Bible verses framed against striking visual images. Check it out for a neat way to reinforce scripture memorization. The more senses we use while learning, the more likely we'll remember, so pictures on the same card as a verse will increase the potential to impress each unforgettable truth on your child's heart.

FUN STUFF

When the world seems heavy on the side of death and destruction, fill your home with more life.

I love the Butterfly Pavilion offered at <www.insectlore.com.> When you order the kit, it comes with live caterpillars. You set it up and watch the life cycle as the caterpillars spin their cocoons and disappear only to emerge as beautiful Monarch butterflies—a truly absorbing process with many teachable moments as you talk about life and rebirth.

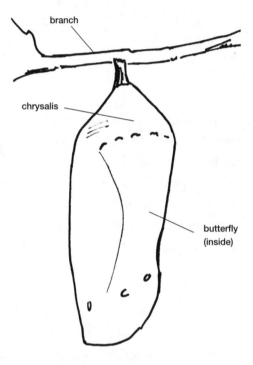

Also, a simple visit to the pet store can be refreshing, surrounded by all the intriguing and noisy life there. A very large fishbowl and a couple of goldfish can provide a lot of entertainment for little ones, or a parakeet in a cage, or a gecko—they're great pets, easy to take care of, and live for 20 years (or as one of my young boys said once when we got one, even 'til he got married). Of course, for maximum involvement, try a cat or dog from the pound. If you've been thinking about it, the timing couldn't be better.

DESPERATE MOTHERHOOD

TWENTY-THREE

Dealing with disasters far away is one thing. Dealing with family disasters—illness, accidents, death, financial setbacks—is another.

But what happens when you come to the conclusion that you're responsible for making a mess of things? What happens when you take stock of where you are as a mother and you don't like what you see? What happens when you feel you've failed, that you made the wrong choices or that you never tried hard enough?

What happens when you feel guilty about the past and hopeless about the future? Because of my blog, <www .mommylife.net>, I'm in touch with many young mothers—and old ones too—who are very honest in their comments about their struggles on their journey of motherhood. And I say "journey" because motherhood is a lot like that, isn't it?

Here's an e-mail I received last week:

Hi, Barbara!

I have commented on your blog a couple times, and your book Lord, Please Meet Me in the Laundry

Room *is one of my all-time favorite books. (Actually, it's probably time for me to reread it.)*

I know you're busy with deadlines, so please don't feel like you have to answer this e-mail right away (or at all).

Here's my question in a nutshell: How does a mom who doesn't have what it takes to be a good mom raise good kids?

I'll explain. I am quite short on patience. I always have been. It's been one of those areas that I've spent many hours of prayer over and yet is an area that I still struggle with daily. I struggle in a BIG way with PMS and/or depression and anxiety. We would like to have more kids, so I can't get on meds for those issues.

I read the first three pages of How to Behave So Your Preschooler Will Too *and gave up when I read, "Stay calm when your child is testing you or pushing your button; anger only gets in the way. Be patient." If always being patient, never yelling, always maintaining your cool, always being able to see things from your child's point of view, always letting your kids help, even when your fuse is short, is what it takes to be a good mom and raise good kids, then I'm going to fail.*

And, Barbara, I promise it's not that I don't want to do these things. I do! I want desperately to be a good mom. I want to raise self-sufficient children. I want to provide a loving, warm atmosphere and always bolster their self-esteem. But my four-year-old whines and cries A LOT, and frankly, it drives me nuts. Depending on how I'm feeling that day, i.e., time of the month, I either handle it pretty well or I just yell at her to get up to her room and not come down until she quits whining or crying. She gets so upset (I don't blame her) and then will ask questions like "Mommy, do you love me even when I cry?" It makes me cry just to write this out.

The one thing I think I do pretty well is apologize and ask for forgiveness when I've blown it. But I doubt that's enough.

So I guess it all boils down to this: How can I teach my child something I don't know how to do myself? I'm horrible at maintaining a routine. I'm terrible at keeping the house picked up and de-cluttered. I do a lousy job of controlling my emotions and not yelling or crying when I'm frustrated.

So how can I expect my child to maintain a routine, keep her room clean, and control her emotions?

Any mom who's come to grips with her own inadequacies will identify—even if the specific issues are different.

Sometimes, and for some moms, the sense of inadequacy is really unmerited. Sometimes, moms beat themselves up even though they're doing a fine job. They may just need to learn to stop being such perfectionists and so hard on themselves. It might help to keep in mind that since our role in building the next generation of believers is so crucial, we can sometimes come under spiritual attack by way of an interior monologue of doubts and putdowns. It's not for nothing that one of the names of Satan is "False Accuser." When you find yourself under this kind of undeserved attack, you need to cast yourself on God's protection and remember all the things you're doing well—not perfectly, but well.

On the other hand, there are times when moms fall short, when those inner doubts are actually based on the recognition of our shortcomings. Then it's not an enemy but a friend—the Holy Spirit—who is illuminating some dust-filled nooks and crannies of our hearts, as though a window had been opened and a breeze were blowing in.

That breeze can actually become a storm that will knock you off your feet and, hopefully, onto your knees. Then you're blessed indeed as God is always eager to offer us a second chance.

People who meet me now or read my books probably see me as a model mother. After reading a while, they learn the truth: though at 21 I got off to a good start learning to be Mom and a Montessori teacher, by 27 I had degenerated into a hopelessly self-centered and neglectful mother, dragging my first two daughters through a painful divorce, crazy lifestyles, and terrible immorality.

At 32, after I had kicked several drug addictions, my addiction to alcohol finally brought me to my knees and made me cry out to God for help. I have no idea where that cry came from, since I had grown up without a foundation in faith. But since I was living in a place where Christianity was very unpopular, and I since didn't tend to trust "church-type people" anyway, I cast my fate to Alcoholics Anonymous.

It was there I learned to live without drugs or alcohol

one day at a time. And as days went by and my mental fog lifted—a fog that had been there since I started using mind-altering substances to avoid the harsh reality of my past—I began to take an honest look at myself.

When it came to motherhood especially, I didn't like what I saw. Though I had made a good start, my dedication to being a good mom had quickly collapsed as I began to run from the ghosts of my own past—abandonment, divorce, a foster home, sexual abuse, and finally a mother who tried to support three kids while juggling her problems with alcoholism and with men, a mother who confessed to me that she never really liked me and had been angry that her firstborn was a girl.

I'm not revealing these things as a plea for sympathy but to highlight the fact that inadequate mothering is something that's passed down through generations. My mother came from a hardscrabble Irish family from Missouri with 12 children and a dad who died so young that the big brothers had to quit school to work to support the family. I can only guess that she hadn't received a lot of nurturing, because she didn't know how to give it.

In the end I realized I didn't either. Since by then I had two daughters aged five and eleven, I might have given up. But instead of giving in to hopelessness, I decided to work to become the kind of mother I wish I had. For those who haven't received nurturing, this doesn't come naturally, but I believe it can be learned.

I started hanging out at the park and watching mothers with their kids, then making a conscious effort to spend time with my kids, to be affectionate, and to tell them I loved them. I began to make decisions that put them first—going out less frequently and, when I did, coming home earlier.

A few years later, I met and married Tripp—a still-single man seven years my junior, who gladly shouldered responsibility for Samantha and Jasmine. Tripp and I were attracted to each other because we were both spiritual seekers, though our focus was on the New Age Movement. Together we built a business and a home and a family.

We had been married four years and had added three boys when our marriage came to a crisis because our spiritual program—based on the belief that each of us is God—did not provide the foundation for a healthy marriage. Headed for divorce, we ended up somehow at a Christian marriage conference where we learned the truth about Jesus—that He was not just a great spiritual teacher but the Son of God. That was where we finally surrendered our lives to Christ.

Tripp and I were sure that it was God who had established our marriage; He had left his handprints all over the names of our first three sons—Joshua Gabriel, Matthew Raphael, and Benjamin Michael—so we just continued building as we had before.

It was then that I began to see my life from God's perspective and to appreciate how unusual it was that though I had failed at motherhood the first time around, I had been given a second chance.

But maybe it's not that unusual. Maybe many of us are offered second chances. And maybe many don't accept.

I'm glad I did. And so I'll tell my story gladly 'til the day I die so that as many moms as possible hear it from someone who really knows—because she's really been there:

With God all things are possible.

Also, for anyone headed in the wrong direction—or who just needs to tweak a few things to become a better mother:

Every day is a new opportunity to make a fresh start.

I guess this is what gives me my optimism, my belief that people can rise above their limitations—that makes me believe that the mommy who wrote the desperate letter you just read really does have hope.

And so I have the courage to answer her:

I so appreciate your honesty. I'll never forget the desperation I felt when I came to grips in 1980 with what an inadequate mother I was. My guess is that you didn't have very good mothering yourself. Is that right? Because I think for those of us who lacked nurturing, loving moms, it doesn't come easy to us to be nurturing and loving ourselves.

Once I got real with myself—as you have done— what I did was try to become the mother I wished I had had. That kept me focused on doing the right thing. I watched other mothers with their children to learn what good mothering looked like. I learned to forgive myself, and I learned when I blew it to pick myself up and start again rather than going down the black hole of despair.

I'm going to be really honest here. You have to stop defining yourself by your limitations and saying you can't do this. You need to make a decision.

Are you a believer? I'm asking because that's the thing that will pull you through. That is what helps you heal from the past and gives you a sense of purpose. With God all things are possible. Really.

I was a horrible mother for many years before I made a conscious decision to become the mother I needed to be so my kids would grow up with good memories and a feeling of safety and security.

Keep trying. Don't give up. It's a process. As you're helping your kids reach their potential, God is helping you reach yours. The first step is an honest assessment of where you are. The second is a desire to do better. The third would be to trust God to help you do it.

Love,

Barbara

 MOMMY POWER

If it seems as if you've had more than your fair share of issues to deal with, or whenever you find yourself in the midst of a painful life transition, you'll appreciate the following story.

The Cocoon

A man found a cocoon of a butterfly.

One day a small opening appeared. He sat and watched the butterfly for several hours as it struggled to force its body through that little hole. Then it seemed to stop making any progress. It appeared as if it had gotten as far as it could and it could go no further.

The man decided to help the butterfly, so he took a pair of scissors and snipped off the remaining bit of the cocoon.

The butterfly then emerged easily.

But it had a swollen body and small, shriveled wings. The man continued to watch the butterfly, because he expected that, at any moment, the wings would enlarge and expand to be able to support the body, which would contract in time. Neither happened. In fact, the butterfly spent the rest of its life crawling around with a swollen body and shriveled wings.

It never was able to fly.

What the man in his kindness and haste did not understand was that the restricting cocoon and the struggle required for the butterfly to get through the tiny opening were God's way of forcing fluid from the body of the butterfly into its wings so that it would be ready for flight once it achieved its freedom from the cocoon.

Sometimes struggles are exactly what we need in our lives. If God allowed us to go through life without any obstacles, it would cripple us.

We would not be as strong as we could have been.

And we could never fly.

—Author unknown

Inspiration

To find the joy in living, keep your priorities straight:

Jesus

Others

You

MAKING A FRESH START

TWENTY-FOUR

From the morning I hit bottom and cried out to God for help until the morning I found a personal relationship with him through Jesus Christ took seven years and four days. A lot happened during that time. As I mentioned, I got sober, went back to teaching, married, and had three more children.

But it started in crisis mode. Getting sober after years of burying tears and fears in drugs and alcohol is just not that easy. And while I sometimes wonder what would have happened if on the morning I cried out to God I had found my way to a church and surrendered my life to Christ right away, I'm actually grateful for the couple of years I spent going through Alcoholics Anonymous.

When I look back at AA, I see the way the Church is probably supposed to be—with people of all ages, social classes, occupations, and political persuasions sitting side by side for hours focusing on the task of staying sober, mentoring one another, sacrificing their time and energy to help each other—for the most part free of judgment and shame.

It was really as though we were all survivors of a ship-wreck, clinging for dear life to the life preserver of The Program. But as Christians, aren't we all like survivors too? I mean, the world outside is so hostile to Christianity sometimes that it seems we should always treat each other with compassion and kindness.

AA was the first 12-Step program, but because of its success, dozens of 12-Step programs exist today to help people suffering from other addictions, including drugs, sex, porn, shopping, overeating, and workaholism—to name only a few.

One of the great benefits of working the steps is that you're forced to be ruthlessly honest with yourself. Although they don't use the word "sin" in AA, you're taught that your survival depends on your complete honesty about your faults. And although they don't use the word "repentance" in AA, they teach you step by step how to be sorry for the wrongs you have done, how to confess them, and how to make amends to those you've hurt.

Doesn't that sound like something everyone should learn? Once you've been through it, you become pretty fearless—which is very liberating. It's when we're afraid to admit to ourselves and to others what AA calls the "exact nature of our wrongs" that we become inauthentic. We begin living behind a false image of who we are.

Every mother needs to know that while there are mothers out there who appear perfect, not one of us comes as close as we would like others to believe. When a mother like me writes to encourage other mothers, it's easy to come off sounding as if I have it all together. I don't. And I think the best teachers let you know that they're sharing their experience—all they've learned from the times they've gotten it right and the times they've gotten it wrong—and their ideals. The best teachers don't emphasize how different they are but how much they're the same.

My distinction is that I've been a mother for 36 years and still have six children at home to finish raising. Also, I was a mother who blew it in the beginning but grabbed on to a second chance and was willing to work hard to do things right.

The hard work started with the program of AA. I'll always be grateful I had this experience, because working the 12 Steps taught me to take responsibility and to become accountable, to repent specifically to those I had harmed, to accept forgiveness, and to move forward.

So when I think of mothers who for any reason have hit bottom, who are experiencing "desperate motherhood" and are convinced they can never get it right, I think maybe I should rework the 12 Steps as a program for mommies who need to make a fresh start.

The original 12 Steps refer to "God as you understand Him." That's because although AA was started in the 1930s by Christians, they used this language in order to help as many alcoholics as they could. In other words, they didn't want someone to be denied the opportunity of getting sober because he or she hadn't yet come to belief in Jesus Christ. I think that was good, because it saved people from dying of alcoholism and cleared their brains enough so they could consider pursuing a spiritual life. This is what happened for me—once I had worked the steps, I decided I wanted to know more about God.

Now, knowing Him, I can refer to Him simply as God in the following steps:

1. We admit we are powerless—that our lives as mothers have become unmanageable.

2. We come to believe that God can restore us to sanity.

3. We make a decision to turn our will and our lives *completely* over to Him.

4. We make a searching and fearless moral inventory of where we stand as mothers—including our strongholds of selfishness and fear.

5. We admit to God, to ourselves, and to another human being the exact nature of our failings and sin.

6. We are entirely ready to allow God to remove all these defects of character that keep us from fulfilling our calling and reaching our potential as mothers.

7. We humbly ask Him to remove our shortcomings.

8. We make a list of all the ways we have harmed our husbands and our children and become willing to make amends to them all.

9. We make direct amends to our husbands and children, except when to do so would injure them.

10. We continue to take personal inventory, and when we are wrong, we promptly admit it.

11. We seek daily to improve our awareness of God

working in our lives, praying for knowledge of His will for us and the power to carry that out.

12. Having had a spiritual awakening as the result of these steps, we try to carry this message to other mothers and to practice these principles in our daily lives.

If you're a mother who's hit bottom and needs a fresh start, try these steps. Take as long as you need on each one, but make sure each one is complete before you move on to the next. In other words, don't try to do Step 4 until you have truly completed Step 3.

After that, you're on maintenance. When you feel your life getting out of control, just go back to see where you stopped working the steps, and start over. Over time, you'll see that it has become an automatic part of your life, that it takes less time for you to wallow in despair, to admit your mistakes, to ask forgiveness, and to move on.

And you'll find yourself a better mother, your family and home will be more stable, and the world will be a better place.

That's the wonderful thing about hitting bottom and making a fresh start—there's nowhere to go but up.

 MOMMY POWER

The Art of Apology

Let's face it: none of our kids will grow up to be perfect. Kids are going to make mistakes, break things, and hurt people—just like you and me. Sometimes it's hard to say you're sorry, but it's amazing how liberating a sincere apology can be. More often than not, it sets both sides free.

Whether you need to brush up on your own apology skills or think them through before passing them on to your kids, here are five steps I use to teach my kids how to make an authentic apology.

- Put yourself in the other's shoes. Have compassion.
- Let go of guilt and pride. An apology isn't about winning or losing.
- Be sincere—no icy tone, eyeball rolls, or shoulder shrugs.
- Keep it simple. "I'm sorry."
- Avoid qualifiers like "I'm sorry you feel that way." They only add fuel to the fire, since everyone knows they mean you're not sorry at all.

And remember: "A gentle answer turns away wrath, but a harsh word stirs up anger" (Prov. 15:1).

Inspiration

To be a mother is a woman's greatest vocation in life. She is a partner with God. No being has a position of such power and influence. She holds in her hands the destiny of nations, for to her comes the responsibility and opportunity of molding the nation's citizens.
—Spencer W. Kimball

Perhaps the greatest social service that can be rendered by anybody to the country and to mankind is to bring up a family. But here again, because there is nothing to sell, there is a very general disposition to regard a married woman's work as no work at all, and to take it as a matter of course that she should not be paid for it.
—George Bernard Shaw

The noblest calling in the world is that of mother. True motherhood is the most beautiful of all arts, the greatest of all professions. She who can paint a masterpiece or who can write a book that will influence millions deserves the plaudits and admiration of mankind; but she who rears successfully a family of healthy, beautiful sons and daughters whose

immortal souls will be exerting an influence throughout the ages long after paintings shall have faded, and books and statues shall have been destroyed, deserves the highest honor that man can give.
—David O. McKay

Motherhood is the one thing in all the world which most truly exemplifies the God-given virtues of creating and sacrificing. Though it carries the woman close to the brink of death, motherhood also leads her into the very realm of the fountains of life and makes her co-partner with the Creator in bestowing upon eternal spirits mortal life.
—David O. McKay

GETTING OUT OF GOD'S WAY

TWENTY-FIVE

Christine's shriek whipped into the room, slicing my phone call mid-sentence. "Barbara—hurry! Your car's rolling down the hill!"

Throwing down the receiver, I spun and raced down the hall. As if something had picked me up, shaken and booted me into a more focused dimension, I could see only the door at the end of the hall, hear only the pulse surging in my ears.

Seconds slowed and separated, like drops from a leaky faucet. Grabbing the only emergency cord I could, I begged, "Oh, God, dear God—please let it be empty."

Moments ago I was leaving Christine's office, my toddler in my arms, my oldest son by my side. At the door we had taken extra time for Jonny to wave bye-bye. When the phone rang, Christine had turned back inside. The parking lot gravel was crunching under my feet when she appeared again at the door to say my husband was on the phone.

"Honey, will you put him in his car seat? I'll be right

back." I turned to Joshua, then 11, everyone's right-hand man. Christine had asked him to come to physical therapy today to distract Jonny from the discomfort and tedium of his workout.

"Sure, Mom," Joshua said. I put his brother into his arms. At 3, Jonny was still too wobbly to negotiate the rocky parking lot safely. Down syndrome meant his physical as well as mental development was delayed. But for his family, his cute little face spelled courage and perseverance. We regarded his features as some would a badge of honor: he had to work so hard for things that came so easily to others. Knowing the importance of early intervention for DS children, we had brought Jonny here weekly since his earliest, floppiest days. You might say we were trying to smooth the road a bit for Jonny to become all God meant him to be.

Why had my husband called that day? Neither of us remembers. He only recalls my cry of dismay and the phone clattering on the floor. Then my screams.

"No! Oh, no! Oh, God—please, no!"

The car wasn't empty. Through the windshield, I could see the top of Jonny's blonde head, framed by his car seat. He was being carried backwards down the sloping driveway toward the two lane road below. On the other side of the road was a 30-foot drop to San Francisco Bay.

As though I were falling down it myself, I felt the agony of what would happen to my little boy in the minute ahead. If the car cleared the roadway without being struck, it would crash down the embankment and end in the Bay.

"Oh, Lord, not here, not now!" I pleaded. Moments from Jonny's brief but difficult life flashed through the memory of my senses. I could hear the beeps of the monitors in Intensive Care, see the tangle of cords and wires from the limp body, feel the tug on my stomach when the doctors prepared us for the worst. So many times we had been through these things, with so many people praying for our special little boy. And one by one, God had healed him of his frailties. For the past year he had been so healthy we had actually begun to relax.

Could God really choose to take him now, after all He had seen us through?

Not if my son Joshua could help it. Horrified, I saw him behind the car, straining his 95 pounds against the ton of metal grinding him backwards. Running awkwardly in reverse as the car picked up speed, he was on the verge of being crushed any second.

I couldn't lose two sons! "Joshua, let go! Get away from the car!" I screamed. Christine was screaming too. Even as we pleaded with him, I understood my son's heart. He always took responsibility. Everything within him would rage against giving up the battle to save his brother.

I screamed again, "Joshua! Obey me! Let go!"

At last, he jumped away from the car. As Joshua let go, Christine and I stopped screaming. The quiet was eerie. The moment hung poised like the last drop of water from the faucet. The car seemed to hesitate, the rear wheels to shift. Now the car was moving at an angle toward the edge of the driveway, losing momentum, grinding to a halt. Almost gracefully, it came to rest against an old and faithful-looking tree.

Bolting for the car, flinging open the door, I found Jonny unhurt but bewildered—he had never been in a moving car all by himself before! Catching sight of Joshua right behind me, he grinned and stretched his arms wide, his way of saying, "Life—what an adventure!"

I've been behind a rolling car before. I've tried to pit my puny weight against circumstances that were way too big for me to handle. Perhaps that's why I understood Joshua's reaction all too well.

"Mom, all I could think of was that I couldn't let him die," Joshua told me later.

"All I could think of . . ." That's me all over, willing to sacrifice everything for some good purpose and ever overestimating my indispensability. Even if I know I need God's help, don't I often think He needs mine as well? Don't I often act as though God can accomplish the supernatural only if I stay involved?

Maybe sometimes He's just waiting for me to get out of the way and let Him take care of things before I get myself hurt. Maybe He would like to do something truly miraculous, something I would always remember, something I couldn't take credit for myself. Maybe He would like me to be more like Jonny, just going along for the ride, a little worried perhaps, but remembering I'm in good hands and ready for the rescue.

I hadn't put my car in park; that little bit of carelessness almost cost me two sons. But God chose instead to teach me a lesson about His mercy and His might. He gave me a picture I'll never forget—one son trying to avert disaster, letting go in desperation and being saved, the second powerless and utterly dependent on God's own outcome.

Because Jonny is who he is, he might always keep that sweet simplicity. And I'll ever be learning from his triumphant trust as he stretches out his arms and smiles. Life—what an adventure!

 ## MOMMY POWER

I'll tell you this right up front: I'm not a scrapbookin' mama. You know how different people have different love languages or different learning styles? Well, somehow God left out any trace of skill or desire to do that sort of stuff when He made me. When I go to the crafts store, I'm in absolute awe at the materials available for scrapbooking, and when I see the results, I'm very, very impressed.

But it's just not my thing—probably because I like to stick to what I'm good at.

So this is a word for all you nonscrapbookin' mamas out there: try words. Every mother is like an unopened volume of stories. You have lots and lots of stories in you now, and by the time your children are grown, you'll have lots more. Try squeezing out a few moments to preserve them in words. Writing on the computer is much easier than laboring over a piece of paper scribbling stuff out, so try to find a moment now and then to write the stories you can tell your family in years to come.

Many moms have started blogs—dynamic web sites where they can share a little each day about what's going on in their lives. As long as you don't become obsessed with blogging, it can be a real blessing in the life of a mom who feels isolated and alone—a real godsend for Christian moms, I do believe.

You can sign up for a free blog at <www.blogspot.com>. But first spend some time visiting other mommy blogs to get a sense of how it's done. You can find links at my own blog >www.mommylife.net>.

 FUN STUFF

Kidnap Daddy!

Plan with your kids to kidnap Daddy. Either arrange with his employer to give him some hours off, or simply kidnap him from mowing the grass on Saturday.

The fun is in the preparation. You and the children can plan the destination, make and pack all the food, then surprise him with a trip to the nearest body of water or mountain or park. Plan all the games you'll play, songs you'll sing—whatever.

When Tripp owned his own business and really thought the world would fall apart if he wasn't there every minute, the kids and I once arranged with his office manager not to put anything on his schedule after 2 P.M. on this particular day. We ran into his office with balloons and swept him out of there without even taking his briefcase or phone.

An afternoon and evening of swimming in the ocean and dinner on the beach.

Yippee!

Anything can happen,
but God will be there too.

LEAST LIKELY TO SUCCEED AS A DOORMAT

TWENTY-SIX

I live with some pretty opinionated individuals. I'm serious. They start young, and they say what they think.

I'll never forget some years ago when my youngest daughter, Maddy, was nine and I took her to the San Francisco Opera to see *Madame Butterfly*. A nine-year-old at the opera? OK—let me back up and explain how that came about.

I grew up not only poor but suffocated with country music and black velvet paintings. (Don't get me wrong—country music is fine, but music is like the food pyramid—you need variety). Though I lived in Washington, D.C., which holds the keys to a kingdom of culture, I always thought plays, concerts, and museums were the stuff of which infrequent field trips were made.

All that changed when I had my first child. I wanted so much to give Samantha the world. But the most wonderful thing was that in giving it to her, I was finding it myself.

Every weekend possible, Samantha and her dad and I donned our tie-dyes and set out early for this or that museum. Then, too, I was discovering music. We were into Led Zeppelin and the Steve Miller Band, but I was also listening to folk and classical and liking it a lot.

Fast-forward 20 years to San Francisco. Now homeschooling, I used that opportunity to teach my kids as much as I could about all the arts. We savored museums, concerts, and foreign films. And theater! Our whole family loved musicals and Shakespeare. You know, kids really do like Shakespeare if they have the right exposure. Think of how people who want bilingual kids introduce the second language at an early age. Before the age of six, the child's mind is like a sponge, absorbing everything around it.

Some people underestimate kids' intellectual capacity. For years, Tripp read aloud to the kids every night—always well above their own reading level. He read the *Lord of the Rings* trilogy, *David Copperfield*, *The Scarlet Pimpernel*, all the classics. All this shared culture was a bonding thing for our family.

For a number of years we even squeezed together enough money for two season opera passes. Tripp and I might go together, or one of us might take one of the kids. This Saturday of *Madame Butterfly*, I had decided to take Madeleine. Though she was only nine, Maddy's voice had the power of Ethel Merman and was always on key. I knew she had a gift, and I wanted to nurture it. Besides, I love spending time with Maddy because she's the most consistently upbeat and cheerful person I've ever met.

The opera was splendid and intense. The plot in a nutshell: a turn-of-the-century naval officer stationed in Japan cavalierly marries a young geisha, never intending to stay, though she's so committed she gives up her religion and her family for him. He returns to America, she bears a son and waits for him—for many years. Simple story, but the music is so emotional and compelling that this opera doesn't need a lot of operatic spectacle and fanfare you sometimes see.

Finally the officer returns to Japan—with an American wife. Because of his chauvinism, he rationalizes away his Japanese marriage as not really a marriage. But having heard of the son, he wants him. He sends a messenger to tell Madame Butterfly. She agrees to give up her son if the father will come in person to get him. She sends the boy out to the garden to play, unwraps a dagger, and sings (of course). Finally, just as you hear the officer approaching the house and calling out her name, she plunges the dagger into her heart.

I felt Maddy tense, and her hand squeezed my arm. She gasped, "Mom, I thought she was going to kill *him*! Why would she kill *herself*?" I didn't have an answer, but later on I thought that wasn't such a bad way to look at it.

Recently she and I took Jonny for a haircut and were startled by the beautician's arms, which were covered with about 50 precisely designed and painful-looking cuts, not yet healed. I wanted to take her arms and cry with her and take away whatever it was that made her want to hurt herself so. I regret that I couldn't overcome my shyness to do so.

Maddy and I talked about it over Chinese food afterward as Jonny tried valiantly to master his chopsticks. And I remembered *Madame Butterfly* and Maddy's inability to grasp why she would hurt herself. I'm convinced that this is one little girl who has her head on straight—not in an I-am-woman-hear-me-roar kind of way, but just with enough self-respect to avoid adding self-injury to the hurts with which others may leave her.

MOMMY POWER

Despite conflicts and complicated emotions, the tie between mothers and daughters is so positive, so strong, and so enduring that 80- to 90-percent of women at midlife say that they have a good relationship with their mothers—even though they wish the relationship was better. This information comes from a Penn State research project.

Family experts agree that the mother-daughter bond is the strongest intergenerational bond there is. Yet it can also be very problematic. Think of the many movie stars—Jennifer Aniston, Meg Ryan, Drew Barrymore—with highly-publicized estrangements from their mothers.

They say an ounce of prevention is worth a pound of cure. Begin when your daughter is young to carve out special time for "girl things." Have at least a couple of traditions just the two of you share, whether it be a trip to the Hello Kitty store, Friday night chick flicks in her bedroom on a laptop, or giving each other facials.

One of the biggest stumbling blocks to a good mother-daughter relationship later in life seems to be mothers not accepting their daughters as individuals with their own opinions and choices. Start early to let go of impulses to control or shape your daughters the way you want them to be. Let God reveal who He wants them to be, and then support His plan.

 FUN STUFF

Things a Mother Would Never Say

"How on earth can you see the TV sitting so far back?"

"Yeah, I used to skip school a lot too."

"Just leave all the lights on; it makes the house look more cheery!"

"Let me smell that shirt. Yeah, it's good for another week."

"Go ahead and keep that stray dog, Honey. I'll be glad to feed and walk him every day."

"Well, if Timmy's mom says it's OK, that's good enough for me."

"The curfew is just a general time to shoot for. It's not like I'm running a prison around here."

"I don't have a tissue with me. Just use your sleeve."

"Don't bother wearing a jacket. The wind chill is bound to improve."

ADOPTION: REFLECTION OF THE DIVINE

TWENTY-SEVEN

I remember when the thought first occurred to me that our family could adopt a baby who needed us.

Jonny, our eighth, was two. Madeleine was barely a year younger and the best thing that ever happened for him. Because Jonny has Down syndrome, he and Maddy were growing up like twins, learning to walk and talk pretty much on the same timetable in those early years. But we knew someday Maddy's progress would push her ahead of him. For that reason—and also since by necessity we had become quasi-experts—we decided to adopt a baby with Down syndrome.

Most people probably thought we were nuts. I was 47, and Tripp was 40. (Hey, we were way ahead of the crowd on the older woman-younger man thing!) But Tripp and I've both learned that when God gives you a nudge, it's best not to listen to what other people think.

It's also good not to dwell on the "What ifs?" or to try to picture the future if you obey the call. That can be discouraging. And I think God probably asks many people to do things that never get done, because they start worrying and looking for reasons not to do what He's asked.

No, the best thing to do is just go with it. Say yes to God, and never look back

We went through the home study process and were just wrapping up when we learned that a southern California couple, surprised that their second child was born with Down syndrome, had come to the heartbreaking conclusion that they could not raise him and signed him over to the State of California. Too bad we didn't know before they signed those papers! Once in the foster care system, a child can't be quickly extricated.

Although I found out about him a day after he was born, it took two months of red tape and lots of squeaky-wheel techniques to be able to bring home our 10th child —Jesse.

That would have been the end of our plan, but twice since then we've been asked—once by the parents and once by an agency—to adopt "just one more" baby with Down syndrome.

And when God has been so generous with our family, how could we ever say no?

When I see the "catalogs" of children waiting for adoption, I wish we could do even more. There's so much need and never enough homes for orphaned, neglected, and un-wanted children.

In recent years it seems to me that there are more and more Christian families stretching and sacrificing to give homes to some of the many children who need to know

God's love. One picture-perfect family I know—3 cute kids, gorgeous home, very comfortable lifestyle—recently brought home a child from Russia, and I hear they're already talking about another. A couple at my church with an only child recently adopted a sibling group of 3 kids. And a mother of 10 (2 adopted) told me last Sunday they're thinking about another adoption.

Will their lives grow a little less comfortable? Undoubtedly. But where did American Christians ever get the idea that our lives were all about making ourselves happy and comfortable? If people are going to put into practice Rick Warren's teaching—*The Purpose-Driven Life* is one of the bestselling books in history—we should now be seeing a lot more sacrifice in the Christian community. Remember his first line: "It's not about you."

Adoption is a beautiful thing. It reminds me of my own former condition as a spiritual orphan and how God adopted me as His daughter. We're privileged to be given an opportunity to reflect that act of mercy and goodness.

Yes, I do have an agenda in this chapter. I'm hoping this message will resonate with at least one reader and that another journey will begin to bring home a child who needs a family. If that reader is you, will you let me know?

Worried about the effects on your other children? I can promise you—the benefits for them will last a lifetime. As they see you translate your beliefs from words to deeds, they'll respect and love you more. You'll see them grow in compassion and love. God will be present in your family in a more tangible way than He has been before.

MOMMY POWER

Did you know there are roughly 34 million orphans around the world? Have you ever thought how blessed we are to have been adopted ourselves? Eph. 1:5 says, "He predestined us to be adopted as his sons through Jesus Christ, in accordance with his pleasure and will."

If you've been considering adoption but worried that money is an issue, here are some things you should know:

A $10,000 tax credit (not deduction, but dollar-for-dollar credit against taxes you owe) is available for families who adopt before 2010. Also, some agencies, like Catholic Charities, in some states will fully fund the adoption of children with special needs. Two of our adopted sons with Down syndrome were handled by Catholic Charities.

Another possible source of help might be your church, especially if you're adopting a hard-to-place child or sibling group.

The Aid to Adoptive Placement program is available to families willing to adopt children with handicaps, with monthly checks to cover the costs of their special needs. While I'm not big on government spending, since the money is there for this purpose, I would rather see it put in the hands of good families who will love their kids. This program is currently not available for children adopted from other countries.

 HERE'S HELP!

Adoption Agencies

World Association for Children and Parents facilitates adoptions of children at home but mostly abroad. They have grants available for more difficult-to-place children (due to handicaps, age, sibling groups) so that families who are willing but lack the funds can answer the call. Visit <www.wacap.org>.

Shaohannah's Hope. If anyone in the Christian community has been a spokesperson for adoption, it's been Steven Curtis Chapman, whose career was in full swing and whose children were almost grown when he and his wife decided to adopt a little girl from China. Now, three little girls from China later, Steven has founded an organization aimed at breaking the financial barriers that stand between willing parents and needy children. Visit <www.shaohannahshope.org>.

And please, if this is the moment that begins your family's journey to adoption, please let me know!

THE WRONG GOOD-BYE

TWENTY-EIGHT

Every mother starts out thinking her family will be perfect. Well, maybe not every mother, but I was one of those who did, especially after I became a Christian and realized how off-track my direction had been.

Tripp and I had five children then—the two daughters I brought into the marriage plus three sons under age four. We were the first Christians on either side of the family and grateful beyond words to have left the spiritual darkness of our earlier lives behind. So we worked a little extra harder at this parenting thing. We dreamed of future generations of Curtis kids and grandkids and great-grandkids, figuring the part we played would be important.

We had heard the story of Jonathan Edwards, the great American theologian, who with his wife, Sarah, raised 11 children. In 1925 Princeton scholar Benjamin B. Warfield charted Edwards' 1,394 known descendents. They included 13 college presidents, 65 college professors, 30 judges, 100 lawyers, 60 physicians, 75 U.S. Army and U.S. Navy officers, 100 pastors, 60 authors, 3 United States senators, 80 public servants in other capacities including governors and ministers to foreign countries, and one vice president of the United States.

Often cited in contrast with the Edwards legacy is a man named Max Jukes, a mostly unemployed alcoholic who lived at the same time, and the family he produced, which eventually included 150 criminals (including 7 murderers), 100 drunkards, and a multitude of prostitutes.

OK, so that's a little extreme. Still, it helps in understanding how two starry-eyed new Christians kept motivated as we went on to have five more children and—as if that weren't enough—to adopt three more. We knew our efforts would have consequences far beyond our lifetime.

This was enough to get me out of bed early each morning for devotions and hymns with the kids, not to mention 10 years of homeschooling. For Tripp and for me, Intentional Parenting was our middle name.

So when, several years ago, our second son left home under a cloud, I was not at all prepared. You know the cliché about a broken heart? Well, it's not a cliché. It's real. My heart actually ached. I couldn't stop crying.

We had seen two daughters married, and I know those letting-go feelings, but these tears tasted different. Someone was missing, and though there were still 11 places at the table, that didn't make up for the one who was gone. There was just this enormous sadness in his place.

It sounds so dramatic, I know. He was 18 when he left. Nothing wrong with that, many people would say. In fact, our secular culture would applaud his independence. But this was not about moving toward something, it was about leaving things behind.

Somehow life went on. Our family passed milestones like the first birthday celebration, the first family outing after he left. It was hard to be happy, but after all, there were other children who needed us to love them and be faithful. Sometimes as parents, you just do what you have to do.

I blamed myself. I felt as though I had somehow failed. My shame and guilt—after all, here I was in the business of giving parents advice—kept me paralyzed for a month until a friend sat me down and gave me a good talking to. She reminded me that each of us is born with free will and that even the perfect parent watched the two children who had had perfect fellowship with Him leave it all for a fleeting desire.

But then there was Jesus. And Jesus paid the ultimate price so that we could once again have relationship with our Heavenly Father—not because we wanted it or worked for it or deserved it, but just because He loves us.

A simple message, but it took time for me to fully understand this as a mother, not as just a nice-sounding theory, nor even as part of my own personal history, but as a reality that will be played out in some way in the lives of each of my children. If God couldn't make his children turn out perfectly, how in the world had I ever imagined that through my own imperfect efforts I could do what my Heavenly Father could not? Was it arrogance or pride?

No, I don't think so. I think it's just that to do the best

job we can do at being parents we have to have a vision. The vision is like the best-case scenario. For me, that meant that all my children would grow up to be strong Christians whose lives were a blessing to others and a witness to the true faith.

It's that vision that gets you through the impossible moments—like kids bringing a running garden hose into the house or bringing home a bad report card or throwing up in the middle of church. The vision sustains you when you're too tired to get up in the middle of the night with a sick child or too selfish to give up movie time to watch something Disney for the hundredth time. The vision is like a roadmap that helps you decide which way to go at any fork in the metaphorical road.

But the thing about visions is that they can last only so long. Life has a habit of changing direction, and so do our kids. We need vision to raise our children well. But we need to recognize that at some point our vision for our kids will be replaced by their own. And sometimes we may not like their vision at all.

But one thing's for sure: we never stop loving them (God never stops loving us!), reaching for them spiritually, and praying for their spiritual growth.

Proverbs 22:6 says, "Train a child in the way he should go and when he is old he will not turn from it."

I believe that with all my heart. The world has seen the return of many prodigals—Franklin Graham, son of Billy Graham comes to mind—and I have faith that it will see the return of my son too.

While some believers suggested we should cut off communication with our son until he came to his senses, we never thought that was the right thing to do. I know my Heavenly Father waited a long time for me to surrender to the truth and promise to live my life by it. I also note that the father of the prodigal son didn't wait for a knock on the door, but the minute he saw his son coming, he ran down the road to meet him.

I will always be ready to run down that road to meet my own prodigal. And I want him to know that deep down inside. I think of that book called *The Runaway Bunny* with the mother who promises her little rabbit son that no matter where he runs, she will follow. God will always be with my children no matter what wrong choices they make, always ready to welcome them back to His loving embrace. And I can do no less.

As for my parenting vision, I've kept enough to give me the motivation, patience, and self-discipline I need to raise the six children still under our roof. But I've dropped the part about 12 happy endings.

The thing is that my son's story is not finished. It takes a lifetime to finish our stories, and only God knows how each will end. My own story is the richer from learning to love when things don't go according to my plan, from gaining compassion for other parents whose children said good-bye too soon, and from the glimpse I had into the heart of my Heavenly Father who, with so many to care for, will never stop caring for the one who is lost.

Inspiration

If a man owns a hundred sheep, and one of them wanders away, will he not leave the ninety-nine on the hills and go to look for the one that wandered off? And if he finds it, I tell you the truth, he is happier about that one sheep than about the ninety-nine that did not wander off. In the same way your Father in heaven is not willing that any of these little ones be lost (Matt. 18:12-14).

A Second Dose of Inspiration

HOPE

*Hope is the thing with feathers
That perches in the soul,
And sings the tune without the words,
And never stops at all,*

*And sweetest in the gale is heard;
And sore must be the storm
That could abash the little bird
That kept so many warm.*

*I've heard it in the chillest land,
And on the strangest sea;
Yet, never, in extremity,
It asked a crumb of me.*
—Emily Dickinson

MOTHERS IN THE HANDS OF A MERCIFUL GOD

TWENTY-NINE

I use time in doctors' offices to read magazines I wouldn't normally see. So, yes, I know all about Britney and Jessica and Nick and Paris. I mean, with all my kids, I do spend a lot of time in doctors' offices!

But last week when Maddy and I were at a specialist's office, I picked up an issue of *Vogue*, which you don't find in pediatricians' offices and which I used to read religiously back in my more glamorous days. In this issue I came across something so interesting I grabbed my notebook from my purse (if you write, you must make sure you always have a notebook) and jotted down some notes.

It was a piece called "Father's Day" by Tamasin Day-Lewis. If you recognize that name, it's because, yes, she is the sister of Daniel Day-Lewis, the amazing actor from *My Left Foot* and *Last of the Mohicans*—both of which I consider must-see films if you can handle a lot of bad language in the first and a lot of violence in the second.

I had never heard of Tamasin, but she is a journalist, and both she and Daniel are children of Cecil Day-Lewis, a

British poet-laureate who died in 1972. What caught my eye was this piece of his poetry that was published posthumously:

Children Leaving Home

Forgive my coldness, now past recall,
Angers, injustice, moods contrary, mean or blind;
And best, my dears, forgive
Yourselves, when I am gone, for all
Love signals you ignored and for the fugitive
Openings you never took into my mind.

Whew! I know some of you who are still struggling with teaching kids to tie shoe laces are way too young for this to resonate—unless it resonates in regard to your own parents. But this is a whole different phase of motherhood for me, although I'm still happily mired in the younger years with six kids 6-17. My older children have moved on to begin their adult lives—marriage, college, and one out as a prodigal. For all the writing available about bringing up younger kids, I just don't know that there's much about watching kids leave home.

It's a bittersweet time. I can tackle my teen boys' room and finally have my way with it, leaving it handsomely ordered and waiting to welcome them at Christmas and spring break. That's a good feeling. Cutting down on laundry is certainly something to get excited about. And though it's been hard to get the entree amounts just right after years of cooking for crowds, there's a lot less food prep too.

But, oh, the house seems empty!—which probably sounds strange coming from someone with six kids still at home, but still you might know what I'm talking about. Even when you have a crowd of kids, you always miss anyone who's not there for dinner.

I had an e-mail this morning from my friend Robin in California, who dropped off her youngest son at a New York college this weekend. She was probably the most supportive sports mom I know—at every football game for years and years (and for 20 years she's run the Pregnancy Resource Center in her town, saving hundreds of babies from abortion). Her son won a football scholarship that will see him through school. She's proud, but she confessed she still hasn't stopped crying. Even when they leave in the best of circumstances, there's so much sadness. Of course, this is what you prepared them for—to be independent—but is it even possible to be prepared ourselves?

I can look at each of my children and see something like a slideshow of how they've looked over the years. I hear their little voices singing hymns with me each morning. Do you know what I mean? I wonder what each of them sees when looking at me, for each has his or her own set of memories about me, and each feels and responds differently to who I am. That's a mystery I can't solve.

And so what struck me wasn't just her father's poem but Tamasin's comments: "One stanza particularly stands out and has always made my brother angry, sensing that our father was putting us at fault and blaming us for not getting to know him properly. I don't read it like that; I see it more as a valedictory, a blessing, an understanding of the places a child's mind cannot reach but shouldn't feel guilty about. It stands . . . as the way I wish to remember the most influential man in my life, my father."

Even if we've been terrific parents, some of our children may grow up to misunderstand and misjudge us. They may spend the rest of their lives denying our influence, but we'll see it anyway and know God sees it too. Parenthood is really a matter between you and God anyway, because it's part of our stewardship. Our children are not our children but God's children given to us for a brief span to prepare them for the rest of their lives.

Will we make mistakes? Of course we will. Think how young and inexperienced we were when we started! God doesn't call the equipped—He equips those He calls. And just like the all-too-human characters in the Bible, we'll live lives filled with the good, the bad, and the ugly. The important thing is to be like David, humble and teachable and quick to repent, rather than like Saul; not to expect perfection from ourselves—because only God is perfect—but to lean on God, to reveal how we can become more like Him each day.

Parenting isn't just about us helping our kids reach their potential. It's about God helping us reach ours. All of God's children have free will, even those with whom He walked in the Garden of Eden. God will not judge us by results—how our kids turn out or how they feel about us.

He will judge us by our hearts.

"The Lord does not look at the things man looks at. Man looks at the outward appearance, but the LORD looks at the heart" (1 Sam. 16:7).

I don't know about you, but I find that very reassuring.

MOMMY POWER

When times are rough—when I've been battling for control of the circumstances and I can't win—instead of giving in to feelings of defeat and helplessness, I've found it more helpful to fight back by seizing control of whatever I can. That can mean taking charge and organizing some disorganized area: a closet, a cupboard, a drawer. It means finding mates to all the socks and throwing away the hopeless cases, cleaning out the refrigerator and throwing away all those stupid little condiments cluttering up the doors in the shelves and doing no one any good, matching all the Tupperware and throwing out the uncooperative pieces that have lost their mates.

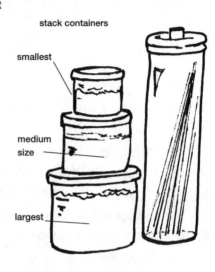

stack containers

smallest

medium size

largest

Maybe it's my personality type. Maybe others would prefer a warm bath. But me, I need to know that I can make a difference—even if I'm the only one who sees it!

Inspiration

Borrowed from AA, which has helped many people stay off drugs and alcohol one day, sometimes one minute, at a time, here's a prayer that can help any mommy deal with all she has to deal with one day—and even one minute—at a time.

The Serenity Prayer
God, grant me the serenity to accept the things I cannot change, the courage to change the things I can, and the wisdom to know the difference.

MOMS MATTER MOST

THIRTY

So being a mother isn't like working on an assembly line, is it?

I know, I know. Sometimes it seems like it is, what with changing diapers and doing laundry and making peanut-butter-and-jelly sandwiches. Sometimes it seems as if the days kind of blend together, and you don't feel that you're really going anywhere at all. Maybe you see an old friend without spit-up on her shoulder, and you really question what your life is all about.

No recognition. No paycheck. No promotions. No raise. No contests or awards or blue ribbons. Just day after day with kids. It's so predictable and unpredictable at the same time—and not in the best sense of the words.

We all have those feelings. I can be your cheerleader for a little while, but you have to learn to be your own cheerleader too. You have to get yourself pumped up and ready to greet every day and give it your very, very best—because your motherhood is strictly between you and God. Isn't that kind of liberating? Everyone else has bosses or customers or someone he or she has to please. But mothers report directly to God.

I don't know about you, but I find that thought exhilarating. And sometimes I put on my favorite get-excited-about-being-a-mommy song, "The Great Adventure," by Steven Curtis Chapman. Do you know the one I mean? It's the one that talks about the wild blue yonder of God's grace and the adventure in store for us when we follow Him.

This is just a song that pumps me up about being a mom! And with all the work we have to accomplish and all the important responsibility God has given us, pumped-up is a great state to be in.

When we find ourselves sleepwalking through our lives as mommies, we have to give ourselves a good shake, open our eyes to what's really before us, and remember this: every moment we spend learning to understand the unique creations God has placed in our lives is new and exciting and different!

Also, unlike the assembly line or an office or any other workplace for that matter, when there's a break in the flow, we can't stop the line and call someone to fix it. Our husband? Only if we're lucky enough to have him home that moment.

Most of the time we're alone to deal with every crazy problem that comes our way, even as the washing machine is sloshing and the pot is boiling and the baby's pulling on our jeans. Right in the middle of all this, your toddler brings a shovelful of ashes from the fireplace into the living room, or your baby tears up all the mail, or your four-year-old rushes down the hall with a permanent marker. Flash-forward 12 years, and the problems are different—

someone out after curfew, a bad report card, a lack of confidence or friends.

I don't know about your life, but for the past 36 years, mine has often felt like a river rushing toward the falls. And I feel like the man in a barrel who's trying to beat the odds and stay afloat going over Niagara.

What's a mother to do? Well, we read books like this one, and we add a few tools to our mommy tool belts. Then when something happens, rather than muddling through on our own steam with techniques that haven't been successful, we grab a new tool and try it. After a while of picking up new tools and trying them, we develop confidence and resourcefulness—our own mommy style.

I said earlier that it's never written, "It came to stay" but always "It came to pass."

That's the good news and the bad news—good news when you're in the thick of it and thinking you can't handle much more, but bad news when it's over and you wish it hadn't gone by so fast.

My prayer is that this book may have opened a new way of looking at motherhood.

Idealistic—not in a way that burdens you with feeling inadequate, but in a way that lifts you up and helps you begin to spread your wings. Remember the butterfly?

Realistic—in a way that lets you know it's OK that you don't feel like Mary Poppins every minute of the day, but in a way that reminds you that the only thing you have complete control of is your attitude. And your attitude makes all the difference in the world.

Try falling in love with your children every day. Remember how it was when you fell in love with your husband and you were so willing to do extraordinary things to show him you cared? I remember once going into the kitchen of the school I taught in and peeling clove after clove of garlic and boiling a chicken so I could make homemade chicken soup for Tripp when he had a cold.

Remind yourself that you do have the ability to love extravagantly. Then do your best to love your kids that way each day. Think of Mary breaking her alabaster jar to pour the precious oil over Jesus. Then let your motherhood be your alabaster jar.

You'll get it all back, you know. As I close this, today is Valentine's Day, and my oldest son, Josh—now 22 with a home and business of his own, planning his marriage in May—paid me a surprise visit with a big bouquet of roses. This was one of my four little boys who never thought much about presents or cards. And now here he is, as if God was sending me a little love note himself, saying, "Yes, you did a good job, Barbara."

It truly is better to give than receive. No one knows that better than a mother. But do we really have any choice? Do it with love. Do it with gladness. Do it with goodness and grace. And then someday you will have survived however many years of motherhood God has in store for you.

You will have done more than survive. And you'll wonder how quickly all the years went by.

The Hand That Rocks the Cradle

Blessings on the hand of women!
Angels guard its strength and grace,
In the palace, cottage, hovel,
Oh, no matter where the place;
Would that never storms assailed it,
Rainbows ever gently curled;
For the hand that rocks the cradle
Is the hand that rules the world.
Infancy's the tender fountain,
Power may with beauty flow,
Mother's first to guide the streamlets,
From them souls unresting grow—
Grow on for the good or evil,
Sunshine streamed or evil hurled;
For the hand that rocks the cradle
Is the hand that rules the world.
Woman, how divine your mission
Here upon our natal sod!
Keep, oh, keep the young heart open
Always to the breath of God!
All true trophies of the ages
Are from mother-love impearled;
For the hand that rocks the cradle
Is the hand that rules the world.
Blessings on the hand of women!
Fathers, sons, and daughters cry,
And the sacred song is mingled
With the worship in the sky—
Mingles where no tempest darkens,
Rainbows evermore are hurled;
For the hand that rocks the cradle
Is the hand that rules the world.
                    —William Ross Wallace

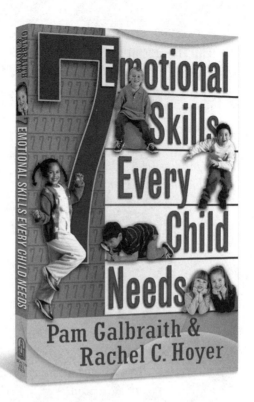

Available from Beacon Hill Press

Learn to nurture skills in your children that will foster their ability to develop healthy relationships with others and authentic relationships with God.

These seven skills provide a foundation for your child to learn to communicate and relate to you and to utlimately worship God and build a relationship with Him. Each skill involves controlling and using emotion to enhance relationships at home, school, and church.

7 Emotional Skills Every Child Needs
By Pam Galbraith and Rachel C. Hoyer

ISBN-13: 978-0-8341-2049-5

Available wherever Christian books are sold.

Where can you find the retreat you need?

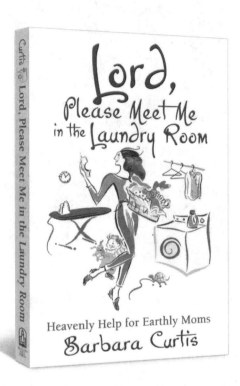

Lord, Please Meet Me in the Laundry Room brings ideas for spiritual retreats into the everyday life of busy moms. This book will unburden, enlighten, amuse, and encourage you in your hectic daily life.

Lord, Please Meet Me in the Laundry Room
By Barbara Curtis
ISBN-13: 978-0-8341-2097-6

BEACON HILL PRESS
OF KANSAS CITY